The
Growing
Teacher

THE GROWING TEACHER

*How to become the teacher
you've always wanted to be*

Jon Carlson and Casey Thorpe

A SPECTRUM BOOK

Prentice-Hall, Inc., Englewood Cliffs, N.J. 07632

Library of Congress Cataloging in Publication Data

Carlson, Jon.
  The growing teacher.

  "A Spectrum Book."
  Bibliography: p.
  Includes index.
    1. Teaching.   2. Motivation in education.
3. Classroom management.   4. Interaction analysis
in education.   I. Thorpe, Casey.   II. Title.
LB1025.2.C269 1984   371.1'02   84-13295
ISBN 0-13-366709-X
ISBN 0-13-366691-3 (pbk.)

10 9 8 7 6 5 4 3 2 1

ISBN 0-13-366709-X

ISBN 0-13-366691-3 {PBK.}

Editorial/production supervision by Elizabeth Torjussen
Cover design by Hal Siegel
Manufacturing buyer: Anne P. Armeny

This book is available at a special discount when ordered in
bulk quantities. Contact Prentice-Hall, Inc., General
Publishing Division, Special Sales, Englewood Cliffs, N.J. 07632.

Prentice-Hall International, Inc., *London*
Prentice-Hall of Australia Pty. Limited, *Sydney*
Prentice-Hall Canada Inc., *Toronto*
Prentice-Hall of India Private Limited, *New Delhi*
Prentice-Hall of Japan, Inc., *Tokyo*
Prentice-Hall of Southeast Asia Pte. Ltd., *Singapore*
Whitehall Books Limited, *Wellington, New Zealand*
Editora Prentice-Hall do Brasil Ltda., *Rio de Janeiro*

Contents

To my three teenage sons—Chris, Jim, and Terry—who fill my life with happiness and my heart with pride. _____

Casey Thorpe

This book is dedicated to the patience, support, and belief of my family—Arthur H. and Helen M. Carlson, Mary C. Paterson, Cynthia H. Damisch, and A. Gerald Carlson. _____

Jon Carlson

Preface

This is a book for teachers and teachers in training. It is our gift to educators who work day after day and year after year with little reward except perhaps the gratification of a difficult job well done.

Teachers are extraordinary people with a deep tradition of persistence. Despite the struggles, the fears, the dilemmas of teaching, they don't give up. They work hard and are paid little for the time and energy they expend. No matter how difficult the task, no matter how high the price, teachers still persist.

No longer are teachers judged merely on what they know. Nor are they evaluated on their teaching methods. We have moved into a new age of understanding. Teachers today are judged on who they are as persons and on their level of interpersonal skills, as well as on their teaching skills.

Teachers need to have a good information base, a sound teaching strategy, good interpersonal skills, and a healthy style of life. In essence, they are *growing teachers*—solid professionals who are healthy people worth modeling one's life after.

Pause for a moment and picture the most effective teacher you have known. Does he or she meet this description?

The Growing Teacher helps teachers to develop the skills to guide others. Effective living principles, life-style planning, motivation, discipline, communication, and problem solving are among the key areas of learning.

We invite you to join us in a journey of growth. This book is based on the theme that effective teachers use themselves as instruments to help others. To a very large extent, teachers shape the values and establish the competence of our children.

We are grateful to the many people who have helped us during the preparation of this manuscript. Teachers, students, employers, office personnel, and the Prentice-Hall staff are among those people who have given us continual riches in the form of ideas and support.

1

Becoming the Teacher You've Always Wanted to Be

Effective teaching requires a sound understanding and command of self, as well as skills in relating in a meaningful fashion to others. In order to excel in work and in life, teachers need to be able to grow and use themselves effectively to influence others. Only if you truly know yourself, possess and value yourself, feel comfortable with and good about yourself, believe in and love the right to be yourself—will you truly enhance self-esteem in those young human beings whose lives are touched by you (Canfield and Wells, 1976, p. xii).

To change others, we must first change ourselves. As teachers develop healthy life styles and habits, they increase their effectiveness almost beyond measure. It is important to believe enough in a healthy way of life to live it.

> *No printed word nor spoken plea*
> *Can teach young minds what men should be*
> *Not all the books on all the shelves*
> *But what the teachers are themselves.*
>
> Anonymous

1

Meaningful education can come only from growing teachers who are *doing* what they are saying.

The Self As Instrument

Teachers and other helping professionals are unique in that they use themselves as the primary instrument of change. Surgeons use scalpels, carpenters use tools, pilots use aircraft, but teachers have to rely on themselves as the vehicle through which to carry out their art.

Values, beliefs, personality, habits, moods, and physical condition influence one's teaching effectiveness. Students learn more from how a teacher acts and what she believes than what the teacher actually says. Think for a moment about some of your former teachers. Do you remember what they taught you or what types of person they were? Seldom do we recall specifically what our teachers taught. More often we remember what they were like—strong or weak, sharing, caring, cold, or aloof, sick or healthy, happy or sad, hard or easy.

Teachers mistakenly view the route to improved teaching as acquiring more and more information to give their students. But students really do not need additional information. They receive much more material in any given day than they can possibly process.

The missing link in most teaching situations is the ability to make information meaningful or personalized. Teachers can provide this essential ingredient through sound self-understanding, positive health, and effective teaching strategies. Effective teachers are thinking, problem-solving people. As teachers put themselves into operation in their own unique way, they deeply touch the lives of their students.

A teacher is much more than a dispenser of information. A teacher is a human being with needs, abilities, beliefs, and goals. Teachers have the responsibility for creating helpful relationships with their students. Teachers must be able to use their own personality and talents to help their students as well as themselves grow. The success of a teacher depends not only on what he knows, but even more on the kind of person he is. The teacher's self is the primary tool he has to work with and, like the tools of any good craftsman, needs care and attention to assure maximum usefulness. While no one can ever escape from his or her own personality, teachers can learn to live their lives in a richer, more fulfilling way.

Effective teaching interactions require that participants know what to expect from each other. This is especially true of people in authority. As teachers make themselves visible, students get to know who the teachers really are, what they are thinking, and where they stand.

Relationships are unhealthy when teachers talk in one way and act in another. Students might be confused if an overweight teacher, lumbering to the lounge, says, "Now run outside for recess. Exercise is very important." Inconsistency puzzles students. They don't know whether to believe the words or the actions.

Authenticity—being openly and honestly who you are—is a most important quality for teachers. Clear messages are essential. Students accept imperfections as long as the teachers are congruent.

The authentic teacher is visible, conveying encouragement and strength. The unauthentic teacher creates doubt, hesitation, dishonesty, and suspicion in the minds of students. It is important for teachers to come to grips with their own feelings, thoughts, and actions in order to influence students in a healthy way.

Self-Responsibility

The way you feel about yourself has a powerful effect on your students. Self-discipline is essential to effective teaching, but it is not possible without positive feelings about self. You must know and like who you are before you can know and like others. Research has demonstrated that acceptance of self is closely related to acceptance of others. Encouragement is the key ingredient.

Teachers do not have to be perfect. It is, however, necessary to have an accurate and realistic view of yourself—your strengths and your weaknesses. This helps determine one's level of competence. Growing teachers appreciate their strengths and work to minimize liabilities.

Hundreds of millions of people are not aware that they are primarily accountable for their own well-being and the ultimate fate of their lives. We live in a society that knows more about the structure and function of an automobile than it does about the workings of the human body.

People continually persist in looking "out there" for answers, formulas, and fortunes, only to discover that they have these resources within themselves. Many fables recount adventures of young seekers who travel the world in search of a noble truth or a priceless treasure. After years of weary searching, pain, and hardship, the aged pilgrim finally returns home only to find the object of the search in his or her own backyard.

These stories apply as much to our desires for health and wholeness as they do do the finding of treasures. Attempts to locate the doctor or the therapy or the book as the magical solution to all our problems end in frustration. Looking within and assuming responsibility for what you find there is a necessary condition for a teacher's growth.

From our earliest years we have been taught that somebody else knows what is best for us. As a society we have given up personal power in many ways. To the teachers in our schools, we have given the responsibility for telling us what we need to know and when and how to learn it; to professional mechanics—the decisions about the upkeep of our cars and machinery; to professional politicians—the right to use our money and direct the military power of our country. Likewise, we have entrusted our medical professionals with the responsibility for our health, giving them the power to determine what our minds and bodies need.

Initially, the general attitude of "tell me what to do and I'll do it," or "you do it for me" seems easier. We appreciate that the training of the specialist gives him or her a special skill. Experts are necessary in all aspects of life. The problem is not that we have experts, but that we often shift responsibility to someone outside ourselves. When we do this, we don't have to suffer the guilt that might follow upon failure. We remember only too well the terrifying admonition, "You'll have no one to thank but yourself!"

To take charge of your own life and well-being implies calculated risks. It means a recognition that you have choices, and carries with it your willingness to live with the consequences of those choices. For instance, in order to meet a deadline you may place yourself under prolonged stress, neglect your diet, and forget your exercise program. These are your choices. If they are short-term, you will probably bounce back easily. But occasionally, they might result in a cold or other condition that sends you to bed. Are you responsible for the cold? Yes, at some level you are. You may have no conscious awareness of it, but you created the condition that weakened your body and made it an environment for "dis-ease." If you are self-responsible, you will accept the cold as an important message from your body, and use it as a chance to rest.

Taking responsibility for choices that result in illness does not mean taking the blame. There is a big difference. With blame you berate yourself for not learning a lesson, or burden yourself with guilt which causes more stress. With responsibility, you accept that you engineered your life situation, and that you can change it as well. You open yourself to learn the valuable lessons that the consequences offer.

Physical Fitness

It is almost impossible to exaggerate the importance of physical fitness. The benefits are truly astounding. Improvements in physical functioning affect many aspects of overall functioning.

Physiological effects. One of the fundamental laws of physiology is that the functional efficiency of any organ or system improves with use and decreases without use. Therefore, all aspects of our being have the potential for improved functioning. Physical exercise and activity have been shown to:

- aid blood circulation
- stabilize blood pressure
- aid digestion and elimination
- help clear skin
- improve muscle tone, firmness, and strength
- strengthen and develop the lungs
- strengthen the heart and reduce coronary heart disease

- facilitate the loss of body weight and fat
- help redistribute body weight for a more balanced shape
- combat obesity
- facilitate physical endurance
- improve posture
- increase resistance to illness
- improve the threshold and tolerance for pain

Behavioral effects. Physical exercise appears to be addictive and, as such, may replace undesirable addictive behaviors, such as smoking, overeating, and excessive drinking. Research indicates that the more physically fit a person is, the more "normal" she appears on psychological tests. Research has also shown that physical fitness seems to affect behavior in the following positive ways:

- helps individuals to work and act with increased energy and reduced fatigue
- the discipline required carries over to other aspects of life
- helps eliminate undesirable behaviors
- improves sleep (individuals sleep better and require less sleep)
- improves self-esteem and self-regard
- improves self-confidence and assertiveness
- improves reaction time
- improves sharpness of senses (especially true with the sense of taste—food and drink tend to taste much better)

Physical exercise tends to change entire life styles. When people begin to exercise, they often quit smoking, consume less alcohol, and change their eating habits.

Social or interpersonal effects. Physical activity seems to be an important factor in developing and maintaining effective interpersonal relationships. This may be a function of increased energy level, improved personal appearance, or heightened self-confidence. The same strategies required to perform a physical exercise or play a game successfully are needed to lead a successful life. One researcher noted that an educational workshop designed to improve interpersonal skills was more effective when it combined physical training with interpersonal skills training than when it simply used interpersonal skills training alone.

Affective or emotional effects.   Certain forms of physical exercise have been found to decrease anxiety and depression while increasing self-confidence, self-esteem, and pleasure. Many writers have claimed that physical exercise and athletics can bring about heightened joy, self-esteem, and a higher state of consciousness. This may be partially attributable to increases in certain biochemical levels.

Cognitive or intellectual effects.   Cognitive functioning seems to improve both during and after physical exercise. There is an increase in mental alertness. One researcher concluded that up to 35 percent of the variance in intellectual functioning may derive from physical fitness. Others have discovered that problem solving is improved, imagination and concentration are increased, and creativity is enhanced both during and after exercise.

Stress and tension effects.   Only physical fitness and mediation have been shown to reduce the negative effects of stress and anxiety. Physical fitness not only reduces tension but facilitates a feeling of relaxation.

The physical fitness level of teachers appears to have a direct effect on teaching performance. Research has found that physical fitness is a better predictor of teaching success than grade point average, teacher recommendation, and test scores. It has also been shown that physically fit teachers have fewer discipline problems than unfit teachers. Many discipline problems occur late in the day, week, and semester, when the less physically fit teachers have used up all their energy.

Teachers need to be models of physical fitness. A recent report indicated that school-aged children get only 25 percent of the physical exercise they need. Children learn what they live. Make fitness a part of your life and enjoy all the personal and professional benefits.

Environmental Sensitivity

An often overlooked area in self-health is that of the influence of environment. Your friends and relationships are part of your environment. The kind of support you receive or the discouragement you encounter affect your effectiveness. Physical surroundings are also influential. Think of your classroom. Is it quiet? Is it comfortable? Is it organized? friendly? stimulating?

You can control your environment and the influence it has on you and your teaching. Match your values and your spaces. Determine what is really important to you as a teacher. Does your classroom express this?

Learning to control your environment requires you to be clear on just what you want from life. Regular use of value clarification and other goal identification procedures can be helpful.

Nutritional Awareness

"You are what you eat" is an often used statement that has much validity. Food today is more for profit than for people. Our society suffers from overconsumption and undernourishment. Five of the ten major causes of death are diet-related.

Although most teachers know the importance of a good diet, few actually eat properly. Consider your own eating habits. Think back to the meals and snacks you have had in the past few weeks and list the foods. Star those foods you think you should eat more often. Add nutritious foods that are not on your list. Add a third category, listing foods you consciously avoid because they are not good for you.

The major diet-related health hazard in our country is the combination of overconsumption and undernutrition. This combined with heavy stress and eating to relieve emotional and physical pain has created a serious health problem. A recent Federal Government Committee* recommended the following changes in the U.S. diet:

*For the full report, *Dietary Goals for the United States*, write U.S. Government Printing Office, Washington, DC 10402. Price: $.95.

1. Increase complex carbohydrate consumption to account for 55 percent to 60 percent of the energy (caloric) intake.
2. Reduce overall fat consumption from approximately 40 percent to 30 percent of energy intake.
3. Reduce saturated fat consumption to account for about 10 percent of total energy intake and balance that with poly-unsaturated and mono-saturated fats, which should each account for about 10 percent of energy intake.
4. Reduce cholesterol consumption to about 300 mg a day.
5. Reduce sugar consumption by about 50 percent to 85 percent to approximately 3 grams a day.
6. Increase consumption of fruits, vegetables, and whole grains.
7. Decrease consumption of meat and increase the consumption of poultry and fish.
8. Decrease the consumption of foods high in fat and partially substitute poly-unsaturated fat for saturated fat.
9. Substitute nonfat milk for homogenized milk.
10. Decrease the consumption of butterfat, eggs, and other high cholesterol sources.
11. Decrease the consumption of sugar and foods with high sugar content.
12. Decrease the consumption of salt and foods with high salt content.

Teachers need to be especially aware of their use of caffeine. There is strong evidence that caffeine has addictive properties and contributes to erratic blood sugar levels. Coffee, black teas, colas, and chocolate—all high in caffeine—should be used with caution.

It is interesting to note that caffeine, nicotine, alcohol, salt, and sugar—the five major substances many people use to relax—are all stressors. Cola drinks and cigarettes, coffee and sweet rolls, beer and pretzels are not relaxing despite their continued use.

Stress Management

Authorities estimate that somewhere between 70 and 90 percent of patients seeking medical attention are suffering from conditions that do not involve a single bacterium, virus, or fungus. These people are said to suffer from degenerative disease such as ulcers, headaches, backaches, coronary artery disease, and the like. While there is evidence of predisposing hereditary factors for some of these conditions, all partially result from mismanaged life styles. Inadequate stress management, nutritional deficits, sedentariness, pollution, and high-risk behaviors such as smoking, excessive drinking, and other forms of substance abuse are among life-style factors that can be controlled. We are not sick from microbes so much as we are made sick by ourselves! We make ourselves sick by unhealthy living. Pogo was right when he said, "We have met the enemy, and he is us!"

At its most fundamental level, stress is any demand placed on the human mind and body. Stress affects everyone, regardless of age, sex, or occupation. Although stress is generally thought of as a negative force that attacks all of us who are living in today's nonstop, high-pressure society, a certain amount of stress is positive.

Hans Selye (1976), the world's foremost authority on stress, has often indicated that stress should not and cannot be avoided. To eliminate stress totally would mean that you are no longer alive. If you make no demands on your body, you are dead.

Stress is the physiological response to all experience. The body responds to stress-producing situations, or stressors, with a series of changes in body chemistry—glandular reactions that result in sudden increases in pulse rate and blood sugar. These in turn initiate resisting or compensating bodily responses. Dr. Selye calls the process the "adaptation response." He claims that continued exposure to stressors that cause significant responses can cause the resistance to wear down or become exhausted. The immunological system actually begins to wear out, and we become vulnerable to a wide range of diseases.

The human body simply cannot be expected to respond constantly to heavy negative stress stimuli without having its blood pressure and heart rate remain dangerously high. This is precisely what takes place within the bodies of individuals subjected to heavy daily stress. Eventually, the hypertension or elevated pulse rate, or perhaps even negative psychological effects resulting from long-term heavy stress, causes the body to break down. Following is a comprehensive list of symptoms that can be associated with stress-related illness:

10

- grinding teeth (particularly while sleeping)
- migraine or tension-induced headaches
- increased smoking
- increased alcohol or drug use
- insomnia, fitful sleeping, nightmares
- irritability
- depression
- anxiety
- shoulder, neck, or back pain
- sexual dysfunction
- chronic fatigue
- indigestion, heartburn
- hypertension, elevated heart rate
- irregular pulse rate (a racing pulse)
- skin eruptions, skin dryness
- spontaneous sweating
- overeating or undereating
- poor concentration, learning disability
- frequent colds or flu
- persistent body infections
- loss of enjoyment in life, apathy
- lack of physical coordination
- skipped menstrual periods or irregular cycles
- impulsive, irrational behavior
- thyroid dysfunction
- forgetfulness
- unexplained pain
- speech problems (stuttering, slurred speech)
- dependence on tranquilizers

If you exhibit one or more of these symptoms, it could be beneficial to identify and neutralize the stressors.

Virtually everything we do each day in our complex society—from driving home in rush-hour traffic to listening to a recitation of the world's problems on the six o'clock news—produces at least some stress. How are you stressed?

How to cope with stress. One way to cope with stressors is to run away from them. Sometimes we can do this. However, this doesn't always work, because it doesn't solve the precipitating problems. It's difficult, and often impossible, to move to a more congenial neighborhood, for example; and usually even more difficult to change jobs. While you can literally run away from some of your stressors, most of them are so deeply woven into the fabric of your life that they are unavoidable. In such cases your only recourse is to do everything in your power to minimize the detrimental effects.

As was previously mentioned, one of the best methods of coping with stress is to maintain a program of regular *exercise*. Exercise dissipates life's tensions efficiently. After a long and stressful day, nothing seems to feel as good or dissipate stress so thoroughly as building up a sweat participating in some type of vigorous aerobic activity.

Relaxation techniques and *meditation* also minimize the effects of stress on the body and mind. One of the easiest ways to relax is to concentrate on and control your breathing patterns; another method involves learning the skill of autogenic training, or systematic muscle relaxation. This involves concentrating on the different muscle groups and learning to relax them. Many people have found that meditation techniques are helpful in reducing stress. Transcendental Meditation and Zen Meditation are among the better-known methods. Practiced once or twice a day, meditation may greatly reduce stress. Meditation can transport you from the place where you are subjected to stress to a fantasy place, or a time when you were once very happy.

Learning to develop *self-control,* or what is often referred to as arguing with yourself, is another way of reducing stress. This method requires that you tell yourself how trivial a particularly stressful situation really is when compared with something that happened to you where you survived unscathed. Because most people have a tendency to exaggerate their problems, this procedure is often effective.

Talking about problems with friends can be helpful because it provides a fresh perspective and helps you realize that you are not alone.

Hobbies provide overly stressed individuals a way to escape the manic pace of modern life. Crafts, stamp or coin collecting, in addition to reading and participating in clubs are helpful in managing the stress in your life.

The causes and treatments of stress are complex and varied. Teachers need to be especially sensitive to the effects of stress due to the nature of their working conditions.

Effective Teaching

Effective teaching requires healthy teachers who model effective living. As instruments of change, teachers must be skilled not only in teaching but in other areas as well. The skills of motivation, discipline, understanding behavior and personality, communication, problem solving, and group facilitation will be presented in detail in the next sections of this book. These skills can only be as effective as the teacher using them. The next chapter will help you develop a plan of healthy personal and professional growth.

References

CANFIELD, J. and H. C. WELLS. *100 Ways to Enhance Self-Concept in the Classroom.* Englewood Cliffs, NJ: Prentice-Hall, 1976.

SELYE, H. *The Stress of Life,* rev. ed. New York: McGraw-Hill, 1976.

Additional Resources

ARDELL, D. *14 Days to a Wellness Lifestyle.* Mill Valley, CA: Whatever Press, 1982.

ARDELL, D. B. *High Level Wellness.* New York: Bantam, 1979.

CARLSON, J. *The Basics of Stress Management.* CMTI Press, Coral Springs, FL: 1982.

CARLSON, J., and D. B. ARDELL. "Physical Fitness as a Pathway to Wellness and Effective Counseling." *Counseling and Human Development,* March 1981.

COMBS, A., D. AVILA, and W. PURKEY. *Helping Relationships,* 2nd ed. Boston: Allyn and Bacon, 1978.

RYAN, R. S., and J. TRAVIS. *Wellness Workbook.* Berkeley, CA: Ten Speed Press, 1981.

TUBESING, D. A. *Kicking the Stress Habit.* Duluth, MN: Whole Person Associates, 1981.

2

How to Maintain Your Growing Edge

Do you ever feel like you're wasting time doing things that really aren't important to you while your life is slipping by? Or do you have so much to do that there just isn't time enough to do all of it? Perhaps you feel worn out, overworked, pressured, harrassed, and never quite able to relax.

Things can be different. You can learn to be more relaxed and happy. You can do what you really want to do by taking control of your life. Control begins with planning. Through planning you bring the future into the present in order to do something about it now. Although most people make occasional plans from time to time, their daily life planning is usually fairly haphazard.

The first step in becoming the teacher you want to be is understanding your life style and how it relates to your effectiveness. The second step is deciding what to do and taking action. You have the ability to enhance the quality of your life. This is a choice. It is your decision whether to grow or not to grow.

Growing teachers determine what they really want out of life. They set achievable goals and priorities and follow them. As they focus on positive attitudes and behaviors, they experience joy, satisfaction, and a healthy zest for living. They become more effective as teachers and as people.

There is a big difference between an occasional planner and a serious one. The occasional planner has unclear goals and often misses the mark entirely. Consequently, the results seem hardly worth the effort, and so he gives up. The serious planner devotes much effort to clarifying goals. What begins as a maze of fuzzy, undefined conflicts, develops into concrete plans.

Every day we make hundreds of choices. Teachers approach decision making in a variety of ways. Think back to a recent decision you made to purchase something. What prompted you to reach the decision? Was it the cost, the quality, the impact it would have on your life?

Our choices are directed by our needs. But sometimes we experience conflicting messages as we work toward a choice. Part of you may be saying one thing, while another part is saying something else. Eventually, one need surfaces to take precedence over the other; thus a choice is made.

The criteria we use in setting priorities may lead to conflict. Once we become aware of this, we are better able to handle the conflict. You may be going to night school pursuing a graduate degree. You may care about your students, want to move ahead professionally, and desire to be a good spouse and parent. When you come home from university classes, you must make a choice. Perhaps the fourth grade math papers need grading, an exam is coming up in graduate school, and the family wants to go on a picnic. If your criterion is the students' needs, grade the math papers. If the criterion is your own professional advancement, then a better use of time would be to study for the exam. If the criterion is the family, go on the picnic. The choice depends on priorities. Regardless of the decision, proper planning will help you recognize the necessity of settling the conflict between your needs and the needs of others. Many people consider planning as thinking, which often turns into daydreaming. Planning is more effective when you *write* after you *think*.

We all have lifetime goals which we think about from time to time. Few people write them down. Unwritten goals tend to remain vague or just dreams. Once you commit your goals to paper and they become concrete and specific, they can be studied, analyzed, and modified.

Imagine trying to purchase an airplane ticket without knowing where you want to go. It's impossible to buy the ticket unless you have a destination in mind. You can't get there unless you know where "there" is. Yet that is exactly the predicament that many people are in. We want to go "someplace." We want to be "somebody." But without a clear picture of where we are going, we will probably end up someplace else.

The basic resource that all teachers have is their lifetime— all the minutes, hours, days, and years that they are alive. Defining lifetime goals is a good place to start your growth process. A Lifetime Goals Statement gives direction to your life. It helps you discover what you really want and puts you in control of your life.

As you set your life-style goals, it is important that they be realistic, obtainable, and reachable with a modest amount of effort. The casual "wing it" technique that works for routine goal-setting is not effective for life-style programming.

While contemplating your goals, think of them in terms of how you see your life starting from right now and from the perspective you have today. The goals that come to mind may be personal, professional, family, financial, physical, or spiritual.

Three questions to think about as you are determining your goals are:

1. What are my lifetime goals?
2. How would I like to spend the next five years?
3. If I knew now that my life would end six months from today, how would I live until then?

In order to have value, apply your knowledge, insight, and understanding. Relevance is important.

List three personal goals that you would like to accomplish during your lifetime. Next to each goal write the date you would like to accomplish the goal.

List three goals you will accomplish in the next five years.

List three goals you will accomplish in the next year.

As mentioned previously, goals usually fall into one of the following categories:

- Personal
- Professional
- Family
- Financial
- Physical
- Spiritual

Go back to each of the three questions and determine the category in which your goals fit.

Planning consists of making decisions. This is best done by first making a list and second, setting priorities. Because items on your list are not of equal value, it is important to set priorities based on what is important to you now.

The ABC Priority System is a simple way to establish the importance of items on your list. Write a capital letter A next to the items on your list that have a high value; a B for those with medium value; and a C for those with low value. Develop your priorities by comparing the items to one another and making a decision as to their importance.

The items you mark with an A should be those that give you the most value. You get the most out of your time by doing the A's first, followed by the B's, and then the C's. You may wish to further develop your list by breaking down the A-items into A—1, A—2, A—3.

You are the best judge of your own priorities. There is no clear right or wrong as to the importance of each item. You may decide that going to graduate school is an A priority while you're thinking about the rewards of advancement. You may later change graduate school to a B or C as you experience the effort. inconvenience, and financial burden.

The ABC's are relative depending on what is on your list. They may change over time. They are not engraved in stone. Today's A may become tomorrow's C.

Although it is not worthwhile to make a big effort for a project of little value, a task of high value can be worth much effort. Effective planning enables you to experience maximum benefits from a minimum investment of time.

We all have the same amount of time. Each hour, each day, each week we make hundreds of large and small choices as to what we will do and how we will do it. As you get your time under control, you will find more time to spend on the things that are important to you. No one is born a good time-planner. You become one as you put time and effort into careful thinking and decision making.

Planning and commitment are essential in order to reach our major goals in life. A teacher desiring to become a superintendent needs to study for a number of years, making a considerable financial investment. This type of goal is like a savings account. You put a little in at a time to work toward your dream. However, there are risks involved in becoming a school superintendent. It is possible that you would put in your time, effort, and money and not become a superintendent. Screening committees and a limited number of positions could be viewed as obstacles interfering with where you want to go. For the three goals you listed as most important, write down some of the risks. Give some thought as to how you might minimize some of your risks.

Long- and Short-Term Planning

Lifetime goals must be complemented by short-term planning. There is no way to *do* a goal. But you can reach a goal by doing activities. Like stepping stones along the way, activities move you toward your goal. Let's say you want to lose thirty pounds. Eliminating second helpings, buying a scale, and exercising daily are activities that will lead you toward your goal. The activities in your short-term plans will help you realize your lifetime goals, designated in your long-term plans.

In order to determine the right activities that will enable you to reach your *A*-goals, be as creative as possible. Quickly list as many ideas as you can without evaluating or judging any of them. Don't be concerned that once you list an activity you'll have to do it. No one will force you to do it. Sometimes impossible dreams become useful. Also, don't limit yourself by the thought that you might not be able to do a certain activity. Quantity and speed are what is important at this point.

Be sure not to confuse goals with activities. An activity is something that can be *done.* If your goal is to be more healthy, some activities that might contribute to the attainment of that goal would be cutting down on sugar in your diet, eliminating salt, reading a book on nutrition, and joining an exercise class.

Take three minutes to list as many activities as you can think of that could possible contribute toward achieving your first A-goal. Then spend three minutes on each to list activities for the second and third A-Goals.

At this point, go back over the three activity lists, devoting at least three minutes to each list adding, modifying, deleting, consolidating, and creating new activities. Let's say your A-1 goal is to develop your artistic talents as a hobby. To reach this A-1 goal, there are a number of activities you can do. For example, you can purchase some art supplies, set up an area in your home to work, spare some time for your new hobby, sign up for a course, talk to an artist, read a book on the subject, or try painting a picture.

Delete Low-Priority Activities

Now is the time to set priorities. To do this, switch from being creative and idealistic to being practical and realistic. In order to eliminate low-priority items, ask yourself if you are willing to spend at least five minutes on this activity in the next week. If the answer is no, scratch out the item.

Don't be concerned about eliminating important items, because you will have the opportunity to consider the items again the following week. It is not necessary to justify your reasons for eliminating an activity from your list. You may not have time to do it. It may be too difficult or impossible at the present time. You may not feel like doing it.

After you have gone over all three A-goal activity lists, combine the results into one list. Set priorities by classifying the most important activity as A-1. Additional A-activities can be numbered accordingly as A-2, A-3, A-4, A-5.

Keeping in mind the priorities, set deadlines for each activity and schedule it into the next seven days. Rome was not built in a day, and neither can a new life style be created overnight. However, each day you can move closer to your lifetime goals by working on at least one A-activity. You now have an action program that can lead you to your lifetime goals. The time to begin is *now*.

Time Management

Time is one resource we cannot buy. Time is life. How often have you heard or said, "I don't have time!"

We always have time to do the things we choose to do. It is easy to deny responsibility for ourselves. However, the bottom line of our life is that we live it as we choose. We spend our time as we choose to spend it. We don't find time in our lives for anything. We make time. We take it.

Time management skills are important in the lives of educators. Using time effectively, like driving a car, is a skill that can be acquired. No one can give us any more time than we have. All of us must live on 168 hours a week. However, we can learn to use the time we have more effectively. We can learn to separate the tasks that matter from those that don't.

Some people don't get anything done because they don't get anything started. Through a study of time management, we can learn to eliminate procrastination. We can learn to work smarter, not harder. The end result will be more time for ourself, our family, our friends, and our dreams.

Pie of Life

Draw two large circles. Create wedges in the first pie based on how you spend your twenty-four-hour day. Consider activities such as working, planning, exercising, teaching, sleeping, learning, meditating, socializing, and being alone. Your pie may or may not reflect the balance you want.

Divide your second pie as you would *like* to spend your twenty-four-hour day. Think about the differences.

GUIDELINES FOR CONTROLLING YOUR TIME AND YOUR LIFE

1. Establish written goals and objectives. Review and revise your goals weekly.
2. Prioritize your goals and objectives.

3. Devote some of your work week to personal and professional growth.
4. Reserve some time every day for planning.
5. Know and keep track of how you are spending your time.
6. Avoid barriers to effective time usage such as telephone interruptions, small talk, low-priority tasks, and inefficient agendas for meetings.
7. Have a daily creative time during which you meditate or just think about who you are and where you're going.
8. Evaluate the quality of your life rather than the quantity. Stop measuring the success of your life by the number of committees on which you serve, the vacations you don't take, or the things you accomplish. Eliminate all the trivial obligations that serve only your ego and swallow up your time.
9. Improve your reading and listening skills. Don't read every word of every book. Read the essence. Don't listen to every word. Get the message from the nonverbal communication.
10. Enjoy whatever you're doing. Build on successess. Don't waste time regretting failures.
11. Keep your watch three minutes fast to get a head start on the day.
12. Set deadlines for yourself and your students.
13. Keep your desk top clear. Put the most important things in the middle of the desk ready for action.
14. Take vacations from time and productivity. Convince yourself that to relax is productive.
15. Continually ask yourself, "What is the best use of my time right now?"

DEVELOPING A PERSONAL GROWTH PLAN

1. *Select one area for development of your plans.* Some areas you might consider include:
   Health
   Profession (teaching/administration)
   Money (financial security)
   Self-development
   Having fun
   Family
2. *Become clear about your life purposes.*
   Are you having enough fun in life?
   Do you feel comfortable with your values?
   What would you like that you do not have now?
   Who is part of your life that you would like to do without?
   Who is not part of your life that you would like to be so?
   If you had a week to live, how would you spend your time?

What is your most important reason for living?
What are five other reasons?

3. *Identify goals and objectives.* Be sure your goals are specific and challenging but also realistic. "I will run in the Boston Marathon next spring" may be expecting too much of yourself. Goals must also be measurable. For example, in order to measure the progress of your health, you might weigh yourself weekly and record the amount of time you exercise.

4. *Determine a time schedule for accomplishing your goal and write it down.* Set both long- and short-term goals.

5. *List a number of goal-supportive actions.* If your goal is to spend one hour a day having fun with your children, you might have a meeting with them to see what they would like to do; e.g., take canoeing lessons together or go for a walk with them in your neighborhood. List both the goal activity and when it will be performed.

6. *Identify some of the possible barriers.* Decide how you will handle them and write this into your plan.

7. *Visualize yourself accomplishing your goals.* List the payoffs you will realize by reaching your goals.

8. *Design a supportive environment.* Choose friends who will help you accomplish your goal. Post goal statements or pictures in conspicuous places to help you stay focused. Provide incentives to encourage yourself.

9. *Keep a notebook.*

10. *Develop a set of benchmarks to let you know how you are doing.*

And finally, define and establish new goals. Personal growth is a continuing process. No one can make you more effective. Only you can do this for yourself. Don't stop half-way up the mountain. Climb to the top.

Enjoy your search for your own unique pathway.

Reference

LAKEIN, A. *How to Get Control of Your Time and Your Life.* New York: Signet 1973.

3

Motivation: Building Students' Feelings of Confidence and Self-Worth

As school professionals, we are constantly confronted with the challenge of motivation. We strive to make potential talent a reality as we work toward stimulating students to learn.

Some educators equate what a child *is doing* with what that child can do. Motivation requires us to look further. Motivation depends on our ability to perceive the untapped resources of the student and to develop techniques to help him or her use these resources effectively.

Motivating students is the most difficult part of teaching. Most educators encounter a motivational problem with at least five or six students in a class. Yet for every five unmotivated students, there are also

- ten who have some motivation but not enough to perform at their ability level
- five who are motivated to perform for the wrong reasons (parental pressure or teacher recognition, for example)

- five who are motivated to try something but never get beyond trying; they seldom stick with or finish things
- five who are always willing to do things as long as someone else provides constant direction and support.

An individual cannot step forward unless he has one foot planted firmly on solid ground. In order to move ahead, we must believe in our importance, our worth, and in our capacity to cope with the unknown. The single most important factor in motivating students is encouragement. By focusing on the students' strengths, their feelings of confidence and self-worth are enhanced. When we frequently acknowledge students' assets, they grow to believe in themselves and their abilities.

Skill in encouraging is a prerequisite for effective teaching. Although many school professionals accept the importance of providing encouragement, few understand the process of being an encouraging person. We tend to assess ourselves and others in terms of liabilities rather than strengths. We have become expert "flaw finders."

Some educators are critical. Others are sarcastic. A few humiliate and degrade their students. Hundreds of times a day, thousands of times a week, millions of times a year, school professionals provide feedback to their students that destroys self-confidence. As a consequence, children begin to believe that they are not capable, not important, and that they cannot do it. Thus, negative self-concepts are formed.

In order to become an encouraging person, most teaching professionals will have to change their present communication and behavior patterns. Rather than focusing on mistakes, we must learn to point out what students do that we like and value.

We are a mistake-oriented society. Consider the tests we give students. The final marks on these exams do not depend on how many brilliant answers the students come up with, but rather on how many mistakes they make. And no matter how much they contribute, if they make a mistake, students can never get a hundred. Mistakes determine the final score. If we want our students to believe in themselves and in their own strengths, we must minimize the importance of the mistakes they are making and emphasize all the positive things they are doing.

Many school professionals believe that they are encouraging students when actually they are discouraging them. For example:

Nancy sat in her chair gazing around the room while her classmates began to work on the new algebra problems. Upon seeing Nancy's hesitation, the teacher walked over and said, "C'mon Nancy, it's easy. You can do it!" Nancy remained detached and thought, "What if I can't do it or what if I can? So what? It's easy."

Despite good intentions, such methods do not produce the desired outcome. Rather than motivating, we frequently inhibit or thwart students. Consider the discrepancies between what we say and what we actually do, as pointed out in Table 1. Obviously, our stated goals and actual practice generally are not in agreement.

Table 1
Our Actions Speak Louder Than Words!

Teacher says:	Teacher does:
1. My students should be responsible and independent.	1. Forces students to perform; does students' work.
2. My students should be good citizens and be respectful and courteous.	2. Talks down to students, criticizes, distrusts, lectures, and punishes students.
3. My students should be happy.	3. Compliments success, but dwells on mistakes; tells students they can do better.
4. My students should have concern for others.	4. Shows lack of concern for students by lecturing, reprimanding, scolding, shaming, using students as servants, talking down, giving in at the expense of teacher's own rights.
5. My students should love me.	5. Demands affection but rejects students when teacher is too busy.
6. My students should feel adequate, be courageous, and feel good about themselves.	6. Does too much for students, implying that they are not capable; criticizes, makes fun of, refuses to allow students to try difficult tasks.

We are products of our culture, which until recently has been authoritarian, highly critical, and evaluative. By continuously pointing out what students do wrong, we deprive them of the only experience that can really promote growth and development: experiencing their own strengths.

We impress our students with their deficiencies, with their smallness, with their limitations, and at the same time try to drive them to be much more than they can be. Tearing others down and exposing their weaknesses does not provide healthy motivation. Instead, it causes people to become less vulnerable and open in the future. Students may change their actions to avoid punishment, not because they have learned the concept we had hoped to transmit. Motivation to avoid hurt, embarrassment, and punishment is a natural human instinct.

Discouragement is the best motivation for failure. In order to do something right, you must have self-confidence. When you think about the mistake you might make, you express a lack of faith in yourself. Consequently, out of this discouragement, you are more prone to make a mistake.

Children need help in discovering their assets. They also need help in assimilating knowledge. Until students feel good about themselves and can relate to material in a meaningful way, positive learning does not take place.

Any information will affect human behavior only to the degree to which an individual has discovered its personal meaning for him or her.

To illustrate this point, suppose that at breakfast you read the morning paper's statistics on anorexia nervosa. Several cases have been reported in your town during the last year. Will this have any effect upon your behavior? Probably not. For most readers, that bit of information represents little more than a foreign language. Because it has minimal personal meaning, it will affect your behavior very little. Later in the day you hear mention of anorexia nervosa and, because you have nothing better to do and a medical book is handy, you look it up. You learn that this is an eating disorder. You continue to read and discover that it is an affliction of teenagers. The information now takes on a little more meaning, and you feel vaguely uncomfortable.

Now let us suppose you hear about a child across the street

who is afflicted with this disorder. The matter becomes closer to your personal concerns and, consequently, it has a greater effect on your behavior. Perhaps you pay more attention, listen more intently, and even kick around in your mind the matter of anorexia nervosa.

Let us say that you are a school counselor who has just read a letter from the mother of a child with whom you have interacted. The mother writes that her child has this disorder and will need to be hospitalized. She asks that you consider the child's potential emotional problems in this regard. The item in the morning paper now has much more personal bearing and produces a number of effects on your behavior. Perhaps you write a note to the mother. You discuss the matter with the child's teacher and other appropriate people. It is no longer mere "information." It is something happening to someone who has meaning to you. Because the information has increased personal meaning, your behavior is more sharply focused and more precisely oriented.

Let us go one step further and assume that you have just been told by your doctor that your son or daughter has this disorder. Now, indeed, your behavior is deeply affected. All kinds of things occur that are directly related to your awareness of anorexia nervosa.

To sum up, the closer events are perceived to the self, the greater the chance that they will significantly affect behavior. This is a basic principle of learning. The challenge of helping students learn, then, becomes one of moving information in to closer and more meaningful relationships to self. Thus, in motivating students, we must focus on two essential aspects: encouragement and meaning. (Combs, Avila, & Purkey, 1971)

Encouragement

In order to effectively encourage others, we must eliminate the following attitudes and behaviors:

1. Negative expectations. Our beliefs or expectations of how a student will achieve have a significant effect on how the student actually performs. We communicate our expectations by word and gesture. For example, when we believe that a child cannot do a task, this becomes a sort of self-fulfilling prophecy, as the student begins to doubt his or her ability. The student undertakes the job with less assurance and there is a greater likelihood of failure.

2. Unreasonably high standards. In an effort to motivate students, teachers often establish standards that are impossible to meet. Some educators operate as if whatever the students do, it is not as good as it should be. Many professionals set standards of performance far beyond the learners' ages and abilities. A student in this type of educational environment learns that: "Whatever I do, it's not good enough, and since I'm not accepted for the way I am (because I'm supposed to be something else), why try at all?" And so many give up trying.

3. Promoting competition among students. Most teachers tend to praise the successful student and ignore or criticize the unsuccessful. Such comparisons, whether verbal or by body gesture, trigger competition. This competition affects not only the learners' strengths, but also their weaknesses. As a result, students often choose to concentrate on areas in which they feel they have a good chance of succeeding and avoid areas in which they think they are less likely to succeed.

4. Overambition. In an effort to be the best possible teacher, some educators demand perfection from their students. This attitude may influence students to avoid attempting anything unless they are confident of being "perfect" or excelling. Eventually students learn to avoid any areas in which failure is a possibility. As a consequence, neither the teacher nor the students develop the courage to risk making mistakes. Neither realizes or accepts that imperfection just means we are human.

5. Double standards. Many educators believe they should have rights and privileges their students should not have. For example, some teachers demand that all assignments be turned in on time, and then take their time in returning them. Some administrators stress punctuality for students but are tardy themselves. There are teachers who lower the grade on messy papers, but whose own desks and briefcases are in constant disarray.

The responsibilities of teaching, dealing with unproductive behavior, and evaluating student performance are privileges of the teaching profession. But by assuming questionable rights and privileges and denying these to students, some teachers convey the idea that the students are of less value.

6. Criticism. Most teaching professionals believe that criticism helps students grow. Sometimes educators actually dwell on their students' shortcomings, clearly indicating that, "You are not OK. I don't accept you as you are, only as you could be." This is a very discouraging and ineffective approach, in that it does not help students grow, learn, or improve. Imagine how you would feel if you were constantly reminded of your faults. People do not feel good enough about themselves to believe they can improve.

We must learn to separate the deed from the doer. Although students do not always perform as we would like, we must let them know we value them as people, no matter how they perform.

> Ruth missed five words of twenty on a spelling text. Rather than the typical response of dwelling on the five errors, we could point out the fifteen words that are spelled correctly. Focusing on the positive gives Ruth the feeling that she is OK. Since she is well aware of the errors, it is not necessary to point them out. Accepting Ruth as she is helps her feel worthwhile as a person and gives her the courage to keep trying.

In order to build the self-concept necessary for motivation, educators must focus on the positive aspects of students' behavior. The concept of self is learned. People are born neither hating themselves nor feeling good about themselves. Everyone's concept of self is learned, in part, on the basis of feedback from significant others. This feedback is experienced at home, on the playground, and at school. It comes from parents, peers, and school personnel. Teachers are an especially significant source of feedback because they provide a steady stream of information that helps a young person form the basis of his or her developing concept of self.

Studies indicate that teachers interact with their classes hundreds and hundreds of times each day. Some researchers suggest that these interactions number into the thousands daily. Regardless of the exact count, teachers' interactions with students take place at a very rapid pace—so rapid, in fact, that most of these interactions are neither deliberate nor rational.

Before school begins in the morning teachers are rational people. They select their instructional materials and plan learning activities. But all day long, teacher-student interactions occur rapidly: "Johnny, go to the board." "Everybody, take out your books and turn to page ninety-three." "That is not right, Mary. Try again." "For goodness sake, Billy, stop pestering Jenny, or I'll have to keep you after school." And on and on. All day the teacher bounces off the class in a sequence of rapid transactions.

Some teachers have a positive style of bouncing: "Good work." "That's fine, Betty. Now explain it to the rest of the class so they can all understand." "You are doing great!" This kind of positive feedback tells students they are worthwhile, they do count, and that they can make it.

Other teachers have negative bouncing styles. They are critical, sarcastic, and humiliating. Their messages tell the students that they are not capable, not important, and that they cannot do it.

In order to feel adequate, students must feel useful and know that their contributions count. Since motivation to learn manifests itself in terms of how young people see themselves, those of us who teach must become instruments of positive feedback. We can help students feel useful by identifying their talents and suggesting ways in which they might use these talents to make a contribution.

A list of positive talents could include such abilities as being

friendly	aware	popular
highly regarded	anticipating	peaceful
thoughtful	strong	appealing
affectionate	sensitive	determined
well-liked	alert	sure

adored	keen	attractive
kind	content	untroubled
alive	comfortable	graceful
independent	relaxed	enthusiastic
capable	at ease	eager
happy	wide awake	optimistic
proud	worthy	joyful
gratified	admired	courageous
excited	sympathetic	hopeful
good	concerned	pleased
inspired	appreciated	excited
jolly	secure	interested
warm	glad	turned-on
daring	brave	intelligent

We help students believe in themselves by believing in them. We must communicate confidence and play down mistakes. We must be sensitive and alert to point out positive aspects of their efforts. This involves recognition of improvement as well as final accomplishment.

How to Encourage

The following points will be helpful in beginning the encouragement process and thereby motivating students:

- Build on students' strong points. Look for positive efforts as well as results.
- Minimize the students' weak points. Avoid nagging, criticizing, or spending an undue amount of time talking about what could have been done.
- Tell students what you appreciate. Some encouraging statements could be "I really enjoy seeing you smile." "I like the neatness of your paper. It's such a pleasure to read." "Thank you for turning in your assignment early. Now I have more time to spend on reading it before the avalanche of other papers hits."
- Be friendly. Take time to listen and show care and concern.
- Demonstrate your liking for the students. Such things as a personal comment, a special note, or an arm around the shoulder convey liking in a meaningful way. Spending time with students during and after class also shows that you care.
- Suggest small steps in doing a task. The entire job may seem too overwhelming. Give discouraged students a small amount of work to do. As they finish each increment, they will feel encouraged.

- Be humorous. A wink, a pun, or a laugh at oneself can warm relationships. Always laugh with students, never at them.
- Recognize effort. Recognize attempts to do a task, even though the job might not be well done. In the initial stages of a new behavior or learning task, students need extra support and encouragement. Once they develop proficiency and begin to experience success, the secondary reinforcing property of the act itself takes over.
- Become aware of the interaction between yourself and the students. Realize that all behavior has a purpose and that often our responses are counterproductive. For example, when a student annoys us in an effort to get our attention, we usually respond with a lecture on inappropriate behavior, scold, punish, or give some other form of attention. This attention actually supports the negative behavior rather than eliminating it.
- Discipline students in silence. Actions are more effective than words. Angry words are discouraging and often untrue. After taking firm action, resume talking with the student in a friendly manner. Conveying the impression that you still and always will respect the student as important. The behavior is what is not acceptable.
- Do not own the students' problems. Allowing students to solve their own problems indicates your faith in them. Give them flexibility in tending to their own concerns and interests.
- Do not use rewards and punishments. These procedures are discouraging and ineffective.
- Accept students as they are, not as you wish them to be.
- Be understanding and empathic. Look at the world from the students' point of view.

Don Dinkmeyer and Rudolf Dreikurs in their classic *Encouraging Children to Learn* (1963) set forth the following nine points to keep in mind when encouraging children:

1. Place value on the child as he or she is.
2. Show faith in the child, enabling him to have faith in himself.
3. Sincerely believe in the child's ability and win his confidence while building the child's self-respect.
4. Recognize a job well done and give recognition for effort.
5. Utilize the class group to facilitate and enhance development of the child.
6. Integrate the group so that each child can be sure of his or her place in it.
7. Assist in the development of skills sequentially so as to promote success.

8. Recognize and focus on strengths and assets.
9. Utilize the child's interests to energize constructive activity.

A THREE-STEP METHOD OF ENCOURAGEMENT
1. Identify
2. Focus
3. Implement

Step 1: Identify positive behaviors, traits, and efforts.

Many educators have a difficult time identifying positive behavior. Table 2 offers some examples of behavior, along with the associated mental health principles.

In order to motivate students, we must have a clear idea of what we would like to encourage and what we would like to see changed. Then we must indicate what this means in terms of behavior, including the required effort and movement.

Sometimes we think we are being helpful and guiding students in positive ways when in reality we are not. It is important to be aware of the pitfalls of discouragement.

Discouraging statements made prior to behavior include

Don't get dirty.
Watch yourself.
You aren't old enough.
Be careful.
Let me do it for you.
Let me show you how.
I know you can't do it.
If younger children can do it, so can you.
Look at how well Susie does it.

Discouraging statements made after the behavior are, among others

No, that's not right.
I shouldn't have trusted you.
You could have done better.
I've told you a thousand times.
When will you become responsible?
If you'd only listen to me.
If only you weren't so lazy.

You did it again.
Oh, when will you learn?
Don't you have any pride in your work?

Table 2
Positive Mental Health Principles/Positive Behaviors

Principle	Behaviors
Respects the rights of others	Takes turns Does not monopolize everyone's time Cleans up supplies after an art lesson Does not disturb other students who are working or concentrating on something
Is tolerant of others	Walks slowly so others can keep up Waits quietly while others complete their assignments or tasks Accepts all children and all abilities on the playground. Helps students from other cultures with English or comprehending school rules
Is interested in others	Includes/or invites others in play Shows concern for absent students Volunteers to help others Talks to and socializes with other students Promotes or suggests social functions
Cooperates with others	Completes assignments on time Works facilitatively in groups Listens to what others say Works with others rather than against them
Encourages others	Notices and acknowledges positive change and good performance in others Focuses on positive aspects of other students Acts optimistic Gives all students a chance when playing games
Is courageous	Takes risks Enjoys novel and different experiences Is calm under pressure of tests Acts enthusiastically toward challenges
Has a true sense of self-worth	Likes and validates himself Acts in a realistic fashion Understands and accepts his assets and liabilities Has the courage to be imperfect

Table 2
Positive Mental Health Principles/Positive Behaviors (continued)

Has a feeling of belonging	Frequently mentions groups to which he belongs (e.g., friends, Scouts, sports teams, church clubs)
	Feels accepted in school and does not need to act out to find his place
	Makes a positive contribution to a group
	Exercises a vote/voice in appropriate activities and procedures
Has socially acceptable goals	Works within school rules
	Is involved in the classroom
	Cooperates with others and is just and fair
	Doesn't precipitate fights and withdraws from physical conflict
Puts forth genuine effort	Tries hard on assignments
	Does homework
	Participates in discussions
	Becomes absorbed and interested in learning
Meets the needs of the situation	Makes good decisions
	Is able to solve problems
	Handles spontaneous situations in a responsible manner
	Does not under- or over-react to assignments
Is willing to share rather than thinking, "How much can I get?"	Readily offers assistance to others
	Shares lunch, pencils, crayons, etc.
	More process-oriented than outcome-oriented
Thinks of "we" rather than just "I"	Uses words like "we," "us," and "our" rather than just "I" "me," and "mine"
	Shows caring and concern for others
	Frequently offers to share

The following list will be helpful in identifying personality strengths in students.

Special aptitudes: Intuition. Making guesses that usually turn out right. Having a "green thumb." Mechanical or sales ability. Skill in constructing or repairing things. Mathematical ability.

Intellectual strengths: Applying reasoning ability to problem solving. Intellectual curiosity. Thinking out ideas and expressing them orally or in writing. Openness to accepting new ideas. Original or creative thinking. The ability to enjoy learning.

Education and training: Any high grades. Improvement in grades. Scholastic honors. Vocational training or self-education through study and organized reading.

Work: Experience in a particular line of work. Job satisfaction, including enjoying one's work, getting along with co-workers, taking pride in job duties.

Aesthetic strengths: Recognizing and appreciating beauty in nature and the arts.

Organizational strengths: Demonstrating leadership abilities. Developing and planning short- and long-range goals. Ability in giving orders as well as in carrying them out.

Hobbies and crafts: Special interests and training in hobbies and crafts.

Expressive arts: Dancing, writing, sketching, painting, sculpture, modeling with clay. Ability to improvise music or to play a musical instrument. Rhythmic ability.

Health: Good health represents a strength. Emphasis on maintaining or improving health through nutrition, exercise, and stress management.

Sports and outdoor activities: Active participation in outdoor activities and organized sports, camping, or hunting.

Imaginative and creative strengths: Using creativity and imagination for new and different ideas.

Relationship strengths: Ability to meet people easily and make them feel comfortable. Ability to communicate with strangers. Treating others with consideration, politeness, and respect. Being aware of the needs and feelings of others. Listening to what people are saying. Helping others to be aware of their strengths and abilities.

Emotional strengths: Ability to give and receive affection. Being able to feel a wide range of emotions. Being spontaneous. Ability to put oneself in other people's shoes.

Other strengths: Humor. Being able to laugh at oneself and take kidding. Liking to explore new horizons or try new ways. Willingness to take a risk with people and in situations. Perseverance. Having a strong desire to get things done and doing them. Ability to manage money. Knowledge of languages or different cultures through travel, study, or reading. Ability to make a public presentation. Making the best of one's appearance by means of good grooming and choice of clothes.

Step 2: Focus on the specific deed rather than the doer.
Although we may not approve of a student's behavior, she always deserves our respect as a person. There is no better motivation than clearly identifying a student's positive behavior when she does things we like. It is important to avoid making statements such as, "You are terrific . . . wonderful . . . super . . . lovable." The problem with such comments is that the student may assume that the converse is also true—that when they do not please us, they must be terrible, worthless, unlovable. As we clearly point out what the student is doing that is positive, she will be encouraged and motivated. This concept is illustrated in Table 3.

Table 3
Comparison of Focus on Doer and on Deed

Action	Focus on Doer	Focused on Deed
A student turns in a neat paper.	"You're wonderful"	"I really like how clear your paper is. It will be easy for me to read."
A student volunteers for a difficult assignment.	"That's super."	"I like the way you accept challenges."
A student offers to help explain an assignment to another.	"You're so considerate."	"I like the way you think of others and offer to help them when you have work of your own."

Encouragement vs. Praise

Many teachers believe that they are encouraging their students when they praise them. Praise can be discouraging and even produce crippling effects. Although praise and encouragement are alike in that they focus on positive behavior, they are different in their purpose and effect.

Praise is a type of reward given for winning and being best. It is anchored in competition. Praise is an attempt to motivate through external rewards. The praiser is really saying, "If you do something I consider good, I will recognize and value you."

Encouragement, in contrast, is given for effort or for improvement—regardless of degree. The focus is on assets and strengths as a means for the individual to contribute to the good of all. The school professional who uses encouragement is not interested in how a student compares with others. The important issue is helping the student to accept himself and develop the courage to cope with difficulty.

Encouragement is to people what water is to plants. Encouragement is internal in that it helps the person feel worthy and can be given at a time when students are not doing well and may be facing failure—a time when the majority of people need it most.

Praise, like punishment, is a method of social control. Overreliance on praise can lead students to believe that their worth depends upon the opinions of others. A conforming child who holds this belief may succeed initially in earning praise, but eventually becomes discouraged. He may be willing to cooperate only if praised and thus will stop contributing in the absence of praise. Also, believing that "I am worthwhile only when I please others" may influence children to make decisions that are detrimental to themselves.

Because discouraged children seldom perform up to adult standards, they rarely receive praise. Should they happen to receive praise and their reward comes, their behavior may suddenly become worse. This may happen because they do not believe they are worthy of praise and feel a need to prove how unworthy they are, or because they fear they can never earn praise again. In effect, they wonder, "What can I do for an encore? I'd better save face by not trying." Consequently, praising a student who is discouraged and desperately needs recognition can have the effect of greater discouragement.

Table 4 further clarifies the distinction between praise and encouragement.

Step 3: Implement by using the language of encouragement.
Teachers can maximize motivation by communicating clearly. Minimizing our own opinions and values and helping students

Table 4
Differences Between Praise and Encouragement

PRAISE			ENCOURAGEMENT		
Underlying Characteristics	Message Sent to Child	Possible Results	Underlying Characteristics	Message Sent to Child	Possible Results
Focus is on external control.	"You are worthwhile only when you do what I want." "You cannot and should not be trusted."	Child learns to measure worth by ability to conform; or child rebels (views any form of cooperation as giving in).	1. Focus is on child's ability to manage life constructively.	"I trust you to become responsible and independent."	Child learns courage to be imperfect and willingness to try. Child gains self-confidence and comes to feel responsible for own behavior.
Focus is on external evaluation.	"To be worthwhile, you must please me." "Please or perish."	Child learns to measure worth on how well she pleases others. Child learns to fear disapproval.	2. Focus is on internal evaluation.	"How you feel about yourself and your own efforts is most important."	Child learns to evaluate own progress and to make own decisions.
Rewards come only for well done, completed tasks.	"To be worthwhile, you must meet my standards."	Child develops unrealistic standards and learns to measure worth by how closely she reaches perfection. Child learns to dread failure.	3. Recognizes effort and improvement.	"You don't have to be perfect. Effort and improvement are important."	Child learns to value efforts of self and others. Child develops desire to stay with tasks (persistence).

Table 4
Differences Between Praise and Encouragement (continued)

PRAISE			ENCOURAGEMENT		
Underlying Characteristics	Message Sent to Child	Possible Results	Underlying Characteristics	Message Sent to Child	Possible Results
Focuses on self-evaluation and personal gain	"You're the best. You must remain superior to others to be worthwhile."	Child learns to be overcompetitive, to get ahead at the expense of others. Feels worthwhile only when "on top."	4. Focuses on assets, contributions, and appreciation.	"Your contribution counts. We function better with you. We appreciate what you have done."	Child learns to use talents and efforts for good of all, not only for personal gain. Child learns to feel glad for successes of others as well as own successes.

grow to believe in themselves is the key to success in the encouragement process.

Phrases that demonstrate belief in the student:
   "I like the way you worked that problem through."
   "I like the way you dealt with that."
   "I'm pleased that you enjoy reading."
   "I'm glad you're satisfied with the project."
   "Since you are not satisfied with project, what do you think you
       can do so that you will be pleased with it?"
   "You look pleased."
   "How do you feel about it?"

Phrases that display assurance:
   "You'll work it out."
   "I have confidence in your decision-making skills."
   "You'll finish it."
   "Wow, that's a tough one, but I'm sure you'll work it out."
   "Knowing you, I'm sure you'll do fine."

Phrases that focus on helping and strengths:
   "Thanks, that was a big help."
   "It was thoughtful of you to _____."
   "Thanks, I appreciate _____, because it makes my job easier."
   "I really need your help on _____."
   "You have skill in _____. Would you share it with the rest of the
       class?"

Phrases that recognize effort and progress:
   "I see you're moving along."
   "Wow, look at the progress you've made!" (Be specific and tell
       how.)
   "You're improving at _____." (Be specific.)
   "You may not feel that you've reached your goal, but look how far
       you've come!"
   "It looks as though you've really thought this through."
   "It looks like you really worked hard on your homework."

To further illustrate the implementation process, Clint Reimer, in his paper "Some Words of Encouragement" (1967) has listed 10 ways of encouraging students.

   1. "You do a good job of . . ." Children should be encouraged when they do not expect it and when they are not asking for it. It is possible to point out some useful act or contribution for each child. Even a comment about something small and insignificant to us may have great importance to a child.

2. "You have improved in . . ." Growth/improvement is something we should expect from all children. They may not be where we would like them to be, but if there is progress, there is less chance for discouragement. Children will usually continue to try if they can see some improvement.

3. "We like (enjoy) you, but we don't like what you do." Often, a child feels he or she is not liked after making a mistake or misbehaving. Children should never think that they are not liked. It is important to distinguish between the child and the behavior.

4. "You can help me (us, the others, etc.) by . . ." To feel useful and helpful is important to everyone. Children want to be helpful; we only have to give them the opportunity.

5. "Let's try it together." Children who think they must do things perfectly are often afraid to attempt something new for fear of making a mistake or failing.

6. "So you made a mistake; now what can you learn from your mistake?" Nothing can be done about what has happened, but a person can always do something about the future. Mistakes can teach children a great deal, and they will learn if they do not feel embarrassed about having made a mistake.

7. "You would like us to think you can't do it, but we think you can." This approach could be used when a child says or conveys the impression that something is too difficult, and he or she hesitates to even try it. If the child tries and fails, at least she has had the courage to try. Our expectations, of course, should be consistent with the child's ability and maturity.

8. "Keep trying. Don't give up." When a child is trying but not having much success, a comment like that might be helpful.

9. "I'm sure you can straighten this out (solve this problem, etc.) but if you need any help, you know were to find me." Adults need to express confidence that children are able to and will resolve their own conflicts if given a chance.

10. "I can understand how you feel (not sympathy but empathy), but I'm sure you'll be able to handle it." Sympathizing with another person seldom helps him, but instead suggests that life has been unfair to that person. Understanding the situation and believing in the child's ability to adjust is much more helpful.

Meaning

Eliminating undesirable behaviors and providing encouragement are important to the learning process. But this is not enough. To accomplish consistent, positive change, educators must work on attitudes and methods that will help provide the meaning necessary for learning.

Effective teaching requires patience. Motivation is a complex process, not a unique event. Its development takes time. Pushing the learning process too fast can actually destroy the possibility of the student's discovering meaning at all.

A common error among teachers is assuming that meaning lies within the subject matter. The meaning of any event does not reside in the event itself. Meaning happens in people as they interact in the world.

School professionals establish meaningful learning through positive regard. Effective teachers are highly sensitive to students, purposeful in their work, consistent, and self-respectful.

It will be helpful to teachers to examine the following areas in order to provide more meaningful learning.

1. Beliefs about the subject. Effective teachers not only know their subject matter well but believe strongly in the material, its importance, and what they are doing.

2. Beliefs about people. Effective educators see others in a positive light. Research indicates that successful teachers see their students as able, friendly, worthy, internally motivated, dependable, and helpful.

3. Beliefs about self. Teachers must feel personally adequate in order to work effectively in their role. Because teaching demands the use of self as an instrument, educators must possess sufficient personal strength to make sharing possible, as well as extraordinary self-discipline.

The giving of self called for in teaching is possible only in the degree to which the teacher feels basically fulfilled. The deeply deprived self cannot afford to give itself away. We must possess a satisfactory degree of adequacy before we can risk commitment and encounter.

Effective teachers identify with people rather than remain apart from them.

4. Beliefs about purposes. Effective teachers see their job as freeing rather than controlling. They work at assisting, releasing, and facilitating rather than manipulating, coercing, blocking, and inhibiting. They are concerned more with large issues than small ones. They are self-revealing; see themselves as involved with others; are altruistic and process-oriented rather than goal-oriented.

5. Approaches to the task. Effective teachers are more concerned with their students as human beings than with objects, events, rules, and regulations. They tend to see life from their students' point of view rather than their own.

Questions for Further Thought

1. How does encouragement affect a student's feelings about himself?
2. Do you have difficulty encouraging some students? What could you do differently?
3. What do you do in your classroom to promote cooperation?
4. How are your students affected by high standards and requirements?
5. Identify some examples of where you recognized effort and improvement in your students and not just final performance.
6. Select a student who seems to be especially in need of encouragement and list as many specific ways as you can think of to encourage him or her.

Activities

1. Develop an "asset inventory" or list of strengths for each student with whom you are involved.
2. Answer the following question about each student: "What do You look forward to when you are with _____?"
3. Respond to the following situations with encouragement:
   a. A student complains that homework is too difficult and too extensive.
   b. A student is worried about and afraid of speaking in front of the group or class.
   c. A student played a game well but lost.
4. Help a student develop a positive addiction (Glaser, 1976) to something. (Examples can be found in sports, arts and crafts, reading, hobbies.)
5. Write letters of encouragement to parents. Suggestions:
   a. Write a letter about improvement in any area, not necessarily involving near perfection. The emphasis should be on the process of the child's attempting to do better, not the product.
   b. Send notes sometimes to parents of students who do *not* present academic or behavior problems. Students who do have problems need more encouragement than do others, though.
   c. Make truthful statements. If you say "Ben is now such a nice child," when in reality he has shown little improvement in behavior, he accepts this as just another gimmick to make him be nice.
   d. Be specific. Generalized statements don't really say much.
   e. In pointing out a child's developing social interest, include mention of how this behavior has been helpful to others.
   f. Transmit to parents positive ways of working with their children. The following example of a letter of encouragement has an introductory paragraph illustrating this idea.

   > Dear Mr. and Mrs. Snodgrass,
   >   It seems to me that many times we have put a great deal of emphasis on things we do wrong or that others do wrong. I have found that looking for positive

things that others do and building on these strengths is more helpful to all concerned than finding fault.

With this in mind, I wanted you to know that today Carrie showed real improvement in her work with the group. She worked very hard at paying attention and responded to three follow-up questions I asked. Because of her cooperative work, the rest of the group was able to work together better, and all gained a great deal.

Just thought you would like to know how your daughter is doing. I'm sure you are quite proud of her.

Many school professionals believe that writing this kind of letter takes too much time. The above letter took two minutes and thirty-six seconds to write, address, and put in a stamped envelope.

If your intention for sending out a letter of encouragement is to get the "little monster to keep quiet," it probably won't work. If you send a letter because you really believe the student has contributed, helped, and/or improved, and that parents and others need to know this now and then, positive results are more likely (Asselin, Nelson, & Platt, 1975, pp. 95–96).

6. Ask older students to be tutors. This helps both older and younger students develop broader social exchanges.
7. Have each student in a group make a booklet of positive comments about the others. Comments about each should be on separate sheets of paper. Collect, collate,and give the descriptions to the corresponding students.
8. Find special tasks for each child—jobs that complement their skills and allow them responsibility and status.
9. Let a student teach the entire group something he or she knows how to do well.
10. Say something personal to every student you encounter during the course of a day—something that shows you recognize and appreciate them for what they are—about their clothing or appearance, a hobby or special interest, and so on.

References

ASSELIN, C., T. NELSON, and J. M. PLATT. *Teacher Study Group Manual*. Chicago: Alfred Adler Institute, 1975.

COMBS, A. S., D. C. AVILA, and W. W. PURKEY. *Helping Relationships: Basic Concepts for the Helping Profession.* Boston: Allyn and Bacon, 1971.

DINKMEYER, D. and R. DREIKURS. *Encouraging Children to Learn: The Encouragement Process.* Englewood Cliffs, NJ: Prentice-Hall, 1963.

GLASER, W. *The Positive Addiction.* New York: Harper & Row, 1976.

REIMER, C. *Some Words of Encouragement.* In Vicki Solts, *Study Group Leaders Manual.* Chicago: Alfred Adler Institute, 1967, pp. 71–73.

Additional Resources

AVILA, D., A. COMBS, and W. PURKEY. *The Helping Relationship Sourcebook.* (2nd ed.) Boston: Allyn and Bacon, 1977.

DINKMEYER, D. and L. LOSONCY, *The Encouragement Book: Becoming A Positive Person.* Englewood Cliffs, NJ: Prentice-Hall, 1977.

LOSONCY, L. *Turning People On.* Englewood Cliffs, NJ: Prentice-Hall, 1977.

MCKAY, G. *The Basics of Encouragement.* CMTI Press, Coral Springs, FL: 1976.

4

Discipline: Using Natural and Logical Methods That Develop Responsibility

Discipline has been cited in polls as the number one problem facing American schools. The inability to maintain order and establish respect between students and teachers is beginning to reach crisis proportions.

The traditional autocratic approach of motivating students through reward and punishment no longer works. Pressure from without is not effective in today's democratic world.

Many school professionals do not know what to do when faced with student conflict or defiance. Few colleges provide courses on handling the child who decides to misbehave or chooses not to study. Some teachers are afraid students will not grow and develop unless driven by fear. And so they use punishment, with the mistaken belief that fear will stimulate

Most of this chapter is adapted, with permission, from an article by Jon Carlson that bears the same title. It appeared in *Counseling and Human Development,* 11, No. 2 (October 1978), 1-11.

growth, learning, and adjustment. Such disciplinary procedures transmit a great deal of discouragement, creating a serious impediment to learning.

Traditional methods of discipline involving punishment lead students to underestimate their abilities, thus depriving students of experiencing their own strengths and assets. Students cannot use their inner resources when they believe they have none.

As we move toward a more democratic way of life, we must unlearn centuries of habit and tradition. These roots are very deep. Punishment fits into the autocratic social system of the past. It was the privilege of the authority to decide who deserve rewards and who deserved punishment. Such judgments were accepted as part of the code of living.

Today we have a whole new social structure. Students have become our equals not in skill and experience, but in their right to decide for themselves instead of yielding to a superior power. Students no longer recognize the educator's judgment as absolute. Trying to impose our will on students is futile. No amount of punishment will result in lasting submission.

Viewing themselves as equals in today's democratic climate, students often refuse to perform when treated without respect. This refusal frequently turns into an open or subtle fight, with decreasing cooperation and increasing mistrust. Some students transfer or drop out of school because they cannot learn in such a troubled environment.

In our efforts to control by using remnants of discipline from an autocratic past, we deny students one of the rights that is indispensable to equality: a say in their own affairs. The whole educational process suffers from problems that center around the issue of discipline. Some highly skilled school professionals become discouraged and resign because they feel that they cannot handle discipline in the classroom. Other educators become authoritarian and tyrannical in an effort to survive. These people become preoccupied with power and control instead of learning and development.

Unfortunately, power does not produce student cooperation. Power stimulates more resistance in the form of rebellion, retaliation, lying, blaming others, cheating, and bossing. Power may also lead to an obsession with winning, "underground" protests, submission to authority, "apple-polishing," conforming, or students totally dropping out of school.

Professionals can get by with exerting such power only as long as students are in a condition of want, need and desperation, helplessness, or dependency. Eventually, students will no longer tolerate being placed in such an inferior position.

In an effort to eliminate authoritarianism, many educators have gone to the other extreme—permissiveness. As a result, these professionals become controlled and manipulated by their students. Consequently, the educators often retaliate by giving difficult tests, developing psychosomatic illnesses, doing a minimal amount of work, or resigning. Neither permissiveness nor authoritarianism appears effective.

America needs discipline to meet the needs of both students and school personnel. We need a system based on internal controls rather than external pressures and threats. The philosophy for such a system has been espoused by such humanistic educators as John Dewey, Alfred Adler, and Rudolf Dreikurs. Their ideas are built on a democratic concept that views people as being worthwhile. They propose a system based on alternative methods of achieving power and authority— methods which, paradoxically, allow more influence in the classroom, not less.

Democracy demands discipline based on principles that stimulate from within. Without such stimulation, most educational influences actually undermine rather than enhance a student's development. Students can be stimulated to meet the needs of the situation if we are willing to resolve conflicts through agreement. The most successful formula is to treat students with kindness and firmness. Kindness expresses respect for the student, and firmness evokes respect from the student.

Non-power-oriented ways of achieving discipline and order have created a new language. The traditional vocabulary of controlling, punishing, threatening, demanding, policing, and being tough is being replaced. The new problem-solving language talks about conflict-resolution, influence, confrontation, cooperation, working out contracts, obtaining mutual agreements, and winning students over.

The ultimate goal of education is to create persons who

approach the challenges of life courageously because they are cooperative, resourceful, and responsible. A healthy adult develops relationships that include effective communication and feelings of acceptance. She is flexible and innovative enough to find new responses to life when old ones cease to work. She can be counted on to meet commitments and obligations. All of these skills need to be developed.

Just as students learn the three R's by being exposed to them, so too, school personnel must teach problem solving, encourage resourcefulness, and involve students in decision making. Students need help to see relationships between an action and the consequences of the action.

Discipline is not an adjunctive technique to be used when the class clown or bully has captured the students' attention. Discipline is not something to resort to only in times of stress or misbehavior. Discipline is not control through punishment, rules, regulations, and autocratic authority.

Maintaining discipline is the foundation of the educational process. The teaching of discipline, or encouraging of self-discipline, is an ongoing process. Democratic discipline involves learning, growth, and a belief that people are able to decide for themselves and accept the consequences of their behavior.

If discipline is educational, students learn from their mistakes. Punishment, which is the imposition of authority, is not an educational procedure. If punishment teaches anything, it may teach the student to become vengeful, to resist authority, and to be less open in the future.

When professionals discover the value of democratic discipline, they can eliminate punishment as a means of control. As cooperation and trust develop, educators will realize that they have discovered a more effective way of achieving discipline. Once educators cast their vote in favor of a system based upon respect and equality, they will experience the joy of success.

Fallacies of Reward-and-Punishment Discipline

The most common means of disciplining students is to reward them when they obey and to punish them when they disobey. This method has several disadvantages:

1. It makes educators responsible for students' behavior.
2. It prevents students from learning to make their own choices and, consequently, from adopting rules for effective behavior.
3. It suggests that acceptable behavior is expected only in the presence of authority figures.
4. It invites resistance by attempting to force conformity rather than learning from the natural and social circles of events. Defiance, sulkiness, and secret resentment usually result. (Dinkmeyer and McKay, 1976)

An Alternative:
Natural and Logical Consequences

An alternative way of stimulating students to learn proper and acceptable behavior is called natural and logical consequences. This method emphasizes the needs of reality rather than the power of adults. A natural consequence is the immediate, natural result of an act, not imposed by an authority but by the reality of a situation. When a student violates the natural order, unavoidable consequences will occur. For example, the student who refuses to eat the "crap" in the cafeteria goes hungry. The student who refuses to wear a raincoat gets wet.

A logical consequence takes place when the educator arranges the consequence, rather than the consequence being solely the result of the student's own act. The consequence must be logically connected to a specific behavior and specific total situation. It should also be perceived and experienced by the student as logical in nature.

When using logical consequences, it is important to keep in mind the following ideas:

1. Understand the goal. As a general rule of thumb, logical consequences should not be applied during a power struggle, because the student may view them as punishment. Logical consequences are most effective when the purpose of behavior is for attention.

2. Maintain respect for the rights and dignity of both the student and the educator. If you fight, you violate respect for the student. If you give in, you neglect respect for yourself.

3. Discuss the consequences. If the situation is a recurring one—such as homework completion problems—the consequence should be discussed with the student, one time only, during a calm moment. This gives him the opportunity to choose the preferred behavior or the consequence when the situation arises. The consequence does not have to be difficult or painful. Most are somewhat unpleasant, but suffering is not an essential part of the learning situation.

5. Always allow the student another opportunity. Giving another chance does not mean he is excused from the consequence. It is important that the student experience the consequence. A second chance means the next time a situation arises, he will have another opportunity to make a choice.

5. Offer choices. If the choices are logical, the student will be more willing to cooperate with demands of the total situation. The choices, however, must not be "open-ended." The end result should be the same with either choice. For example, "Do you want to talk to me about your test results now or in five minutes?" "Would you like to clean up your area now or after school?" "I'm sorry, but we don't run and yell in school. Would you like to settle down inside, or would you rather go outside and do your running?"

6. Avoid punitive undertones. There should be no stated or implied implications of superiority or moral judgments regarding the student. Impatience, ridicule, humiliation, shame, and retaliation give the child a reason to punish in return. The student may learn that being powerful is the safest way to deal with people.

7. Expect the best. The implicit attitude, which may or not be expressed, should be one of mild regret that the student has chosen the action leading to the consequence. You may wish to indicate that you expect the student next time to choose a behavior more in accord with the reality of the situation.

The purpose of discipline is to teach students how to get along properly in the social world. Logical consequences allow students to learn about and from the logical reality of the situation. As students experience consequences that are logically related to their behavior, they come to understand the importance of mutual rights and mutual respect. When consequences "fit" the behavior, students often learn discipline quickly.

Logical Consequences vs. Punishment: A Comparison

In order to use logical consequences effectively, the school professional must have a clear understanding of this method of discipline. The following discussion compares the principles of logical consequences with those of punishment.

Logical consequences express the reality of the social order; punishment expresses the power of personal authority. The social order establishes the rules for living that we all must learn in order to function effectively in society. Logical consequences deal with the presenting *situation* and what the student needs to learn. This is a situation-centered form of discipline. Punishment is concerned more with making the student act in the way deemed appropriate. This is self-centered discipline.

> *Situation:* Rick is walking around pestering the other kids through touching, noise-making, and hand and body gestures.
> *Adult using punishment:* "Rick, sit down! Stop bothering the other kids!"
> *Adult using logical consequences:* "Rick, you have a choice. You may sit down and act properly, or you may go to the principal's office. You decide."

Logical consequences are related to the misbehavior; punishment is arbitrary and seldom is logically related to the situation. In terms of application, the consequence must be logically connected to the misbehavior. The student must understand the relationship between action and the subsequent consequence as a result of personal behavior rather than the behavior of others. If he does not clearly see this, he will view the adult's act as punishment rather than consequence.

For example, two children are fighting on the playground rather than participating in a group activity. If the teacher orders the children to sit on the bench for the rest of the period, they may be so antagonized by the command that they fail to see the corrective intent. The learning experience would be more effective if the teacher were to say calmly, "I see you do not want to play the game like the rest of the group. Therefore, please sit on the bench until you feel you are ready to play properly." In this way, the teacher is removed from the authority role by relating the result of the students' action to what they are doing, not to what they have done. This also provides the students an opportunity to return to the group by altering their behavior.

Although there is no guarantee that the students initially will accept this action as purely corrective, the chances of effective learning are great. It is important to clearly instruct the students in how their behavior results in the consequences. The students then realize they have a choice—appropriate or inappropriate behavior and the consequences of each.

> *Adult using punishment:* "Frank! I've told you before to stop writing on the desk. You'll have to stay after school for a week."
> *Adult using logical consequences:* "Frank, I see that you have chosen to keep writing on the desk. Since you are unable to use a desk properly, you can use just the chair. Please put your desk against the wall until you feel you can use it properly and would like to try again."

Logical consequences are impersonal and imply no element of personal moral judgment; punishment is personalized and implies moral judgment. We tend to see children who agree with us and conform to all rules as good, and those who disagree and violate rules as bad. By equating worth with being good, many educators use moral judgment as a means of maintaining the power of an authority figure while correcting misbehavior.

The concept on which logical consequences is based presupposes that children are born neither good nor bad, nor that they develop in either direction. Although an individual's acts may be judged good or bad by society, the person's essential value as a human being is not altered. It is important for the teacher to point out that the student's acts of misbehavior are mistakes rather than sins.

The logical consequence distinguishes between the deed and the doer, making no judgments. Logical and natural consequences give students the choice of deciding for themselves whether or not they want to repeat a given act. Once they experience the unpleasant consequences of their acts, they are apt to choose to avoid that behavior in the future. This type of discipline relieves students from feeling they are subject to the whim of an authority over which they have no control.

> *Adult using punishment (angrily):* "You took my ruler again without permission! Don't you know that's like stealing? You know stealing is wrong! And now you've lost it! You're to stay after school for two weeks!"
>
> *Adult using logical consequences:* "How will you replace the ruler?" (Focuses on the impersonal fact that the ruler must be replaced, rather than imposing a moral judgment on the act of stealing.)

Logical consequences are concerned with present and future behavior; punishment is concerned with past behavior. Punishment is imposed for past transgressions. Consequences come into play only when the student disregards order. There is no element of "sin" or "penance" involved in consequences. Once the student learns that an unpleasant result inevitably follows an antisocial act, he usually thinks twice before repeating the act. Thus, order and reality itself, rather than the arbitrary power of an adult, bring about unpleasant consequences. This method allows teachers to stand by as friends, because the student does not feel personally defeated.

Because of the fear of punishment, many students do not develop comfortable and mutually rewarding relationships with school personnel. Sarcasm, ridicule, and humiliation often hurt as much as or more than the paddle. The pain of punishment can be emotional as well as physical. Neither is effective.

> *Adult using punishment (angrily):* "Sam! Again there is no homework from you. You never turn in homework. Yesterday you didn't even have an excuse. You can just stay after school every day for three weeks."
>
> *Adult using consequences:* "I'm sorry, Sam, but it seems as though you can't take responsibility for completing your homework outside of school. Today I want you to finish all your homework in school before leaving."

In logical consequences the voice is friendly and implies good will; in punishment the voice threatens the "offender" with disrespect and seldom is friendly. One cannot conceal one's real attitude. The voice is a true barometer, indicating open or underlying attitudes. A critical and punitive voice can turn consequences into punishments. If consequences are designed as retaliation, as in the assumption "this will teach you a lesson," they become ineffective. Teachers who feel personally involved, threatened, or defeated are in no position to apply logical consequences.

The application of consequences presupposes that the adult take the role of a friendly bystander. A harsh tone belies any assumption of friendliness. It connotes demands, anger, pressure, or retaliation, which are all foreign to the application of logical consequences.

Punishment demands obedience. Logical consequences permit choice. Anger, warnings, threats, and reminders may turn a consequence into a punishment. Some educators control the verbal expression of hostility but continue to communicate it nonverbally—"shouting with their mouths shut." Hidden motives such as power can turn consequences into emotional punishment.

The most effective teachers are those who view misbehavior as a learning experience rather than a violation of authority. Remaining matter-of-fact and nonpunishing is extremely important. This means separating the deed from the doer. Those who regard misbehavior objectively, rather than as a personal affront, have the most success with this method of discipline.

Basic Principles of Natural and Logical Consequences

If we allow students to experience the consequences of their acts, we provide an honest and real learning situation. The following principles are guides to the effective use of natural and logical consequences. (Dinkmeyer and McKay, 1976)

Understand the student's goal. Logical consequences, which result from letting the student experience the reality of society, are most appropriate for attention-getting behavior. If the student's goal is power or revenge, the consequence may be viewed as arbitrary punishment. In such a situation, it is important for the teacher to work on the relationship with the student through respect and encouragement, postponing consequences until a healthy relationship is established.

Be both firm and kind. Effective adults are firm and kind in their discipline. Firmness should not be interpreted as strictness or harshness. Strictness relates to control of the student. Firmness is an attitude dealing with our own behavior or feelings.

Refrain from overprotecting. The student should be allowed to experience the consequences of his or her own choices. Avoid taking responsibilities which are logically those of the student. Overprotection deprives students of the experience of their own strength.

Be consistent in your actions. As a part of order, consistency helps establish boundaries and limitations that provide security. Training methods that are applied haphazardly are not effective. As consistency is increased, students know what to expect and can make their decisions accordingly.

Separate the deed from the doer. Your tone of voice and nonverbal behavior can indicate that the student is accepted and respected even when his or her behavior is not acceptable. Failure to show respect for the student turns consequences into punishment. Teachers must base their actions on the student's deeds, while continuing to respect them as persons.

Encourage self-reliance and independence. Don't do for your students what they can do for themselves. Independence prepares students for happy, responsible adulthood. The more school personnel allow students to become self-reliant, the more competent the students will feel.

Avoid pity. Pity is a damaging attitude because it tells recipients they are somehow defective—that they can't handle problems. Protecting students from responsibilities because we feel sorry for them gives them the impression that life owes them something and that they have the right to demand more and more. Such an attitude greatly undermines the student's ability to participate and contribute. Pity may also teach that adult authority figures don't really mean what they say. Although overprotection may serve to make an insecure adult feel stronger, it does so at the child's expense. Pity is not the same as empathy. Because we care about our students, we want them to know that we empathize with them and understand their feelings. This provides strength, whereas pity promotes weakness.

Refuse to become overconcerned about what others think. Some professionals hesitate to allow students to experience the consequences of their behavior because they fear disapproval from their colleagues or administrators. Students are independent individuals who must learn to decide how they will behave. The behavior of a student does not necessarily reflect on the authority figure as a person or professional. Educators cannot be expected to be responsible for the behavior of their students.

Recognize who owns the problem. Schools assume ownership of many problems that actually belong to the student. It is important to define the problem, decide to whom it belongs, and to act accordingly.

Talk less and act more. We hinder our effectiveness by talking too much. A student easily becomes "deaf." Because students are more willing to listen when they are on friendly terms with the teacher, most talking should take place under such conditions. When using logical consequences, talk should be kept to a minimum as the adult follows through with action.

Refuse to fight or give in. The school professional does not have to "win." This is not a contest. The goal is to help the student become responsible for his or her behavior. The educator must be willing to accept the student's decision on how to respond to limits.

Let all students share responsibility. When an incident occurs involving a group of students, there is no need to try to find the guilty party. Faultfinding only increases rivalry. All should share the responsibility and be allowed to decide how to handle the problem. Ignore tattling.

It is helpful to be aware of some of the pitfalls one might encounter in using logical consequences.

1. If you're inconsistent and don't follow through, you teach the child to disregard what the adult says. Inconsistency subordinates order in the classroom to the teacher's momentary feelings.

2. You will have difficulty in working on more than one behavior at a time. This is especially true if the teacher is displeased with the way the student responds to the consequence by not demonstrating enough misery or by trying to get out of it. The positive possibilities of the consequence may be cancelled by the unwitting reinforcement of the student's mistaken goal.

3. If you feel guilty, you may teach the student that it pays to feel abused if the teacher feels guilty.

4. You may think it seems easier to punish or overlook than to take the time and thought to initiate logical consequences and carry them through. But giving way to expediency interferes with successful discipline.

5. Don't expect standards of behavior from the student that are not expected of the school professional.

6. Rubbing it in ("I told you so") increases the student's anger. Consequently, the student is less likely to cooperate willingly with the total situation and to assess the consequences as logical.

7. Don't use consequences in a dangerous situation. Action rather than consequence is needed in such a circumstance.

School can be enjoyable for students. School can be a place for young people to use their minds to learn necessary skills and to deal with relevant issues. Ideally, school is a place with warm, caring people who are willing to become involved. Unless the school is a basically enjoyable place, there is no point in worrying about discipline. If the students don't want to be there and are there only because the law says they must be, the preconditions exist for a power struggle in which no one will win.

An Ounce of Prevention

Before discussing procedures to combat existing misbehavior, it is important to examine procedures that actually prevent misbehavior and facilitate healthy behavior.

Avoid reinforcing or provoking misbehavior. A student has motives for misbehaving. It is best to avoid doing what the student expects, for that may be his goal. When the student discovers that the school professional is not falling into his trap, the misbehavior becomes less rewarding. The teacher can then concentrate on encouraging active/constructive behavior.

Develop a relationship of mutual respect by being kind and firm. Kindness shows respect for the student, and firmness shows respect for oneself. Students respect adults who say what they mean and mean what they say. Do not make threats you cannot carry out. When conflict looms, it is unnecessary to fight, but do not give in or compromise your position.

Look for assets in each student. Encouragement is an essential skill in building the student's self-esteem and feelings of success. Inventory each student's talents, assets, and strengths. These may include traits such as cooperativeness, persistence, and loyalty, as well as superior skills. These assets and strengths can become the focus of a healthy relationship and enable the educator to encourage and value.

Some school professionals become discouraged when working with students in need of special discipline. Remarks such as, "I don't know what to do with this kid," or, "Everytime I try to . . . he does something different," are clues to a discouraged adult. Learning to encourage oneself and others is the key ingredient in bringing about more cooperative behavior.

Be flexible in your attitude toward the student. Misbehaving students are discouraged in the sense that they feel they can't belong and be accepted. They find their place through passive or destructive behavior. Sometimes teachers anticipate trouble from a student and in turn tend to bring about the undesirable behavior. Since expectations of others are powerful motives, it is advantageous for the educator to act as if the student will cooperate. Chances are that the student will live up to these expectations.

Systematic Procedure
for Using Consequences
(Dinkmeyer and McKay, 1976)

Step 1: Provide choices.
Choice is essential in the use of logical consequences. The adult proposes alternatives and the student makes a choice. The adult must accept the student's decision with an attitude of respect.

The following are examples of choices phrased in a respectful manner:

> "Jennifer, we are trying to watch the movie. You may settle down and watch it with us or leave the room. You decide which you'd rather do."

> "I'm willing to accept all assignments that are typewritten and turned in by next Friday."

A fourth grade boy had been in the habit of tipping his chair back while sitting in the classroom. Despite the fact that he had fallen back onto the floor, he insisted on continuing this attention-getting device. Finally, the teacher asked him if he would prefer to lean back in the chair rather than sit upright. The teacher placed books under the front legs of the chair so he was leaning back in an uncomfortable, but not dangerous, position. The boy then was asked to maintain the position until he decided to sit properly. Before long, he removed the books and no further episode of tipping back his chair has occurred.

Step 2: As you follow through with a consequence, give assurance of an opportunity to change the decision later.
After students have been given a choice they often decide to test the limits. Should this occur, the adult can tell them that the decision stands, but they may try again later.

> *Adult (following through matter-of-factly):* "I see you haven't stopped talking, so I assume you've decided to leave the room and go to the principal's office. Come back when you feel that you can work quietly."

Step 3: If the misbehavior is repeated, extend the time that must elapse before the student may try again.
Students who continue to misbehave are saying they are not ready, or have not learned, to be responsible.

> "I see that you still have not decided to stop talking in the classroom and have decided to go to the principal's office again. You may try again tomorrow."

From this point on, the adult should use no words except to assure the student of another opportunity to try again. It is important to state the time, which should be increased again, at which the student will have another opportunity.

"You may try again in three days."

If there is further difficulty, check the steps involved to be sure the principles are understood clearly. Be sure the action is an expression of logical consequences rather than punishment.
To reiterate

- Show an "open" attitude; give the student a choice and accept the student's decision.
- Use a friendly tone of voice that expresses good will.
- Make sure the consequence is logically related to the misbehavior.

Dealing with Misbehavior

The following points illustrate how logical consequences are used in dealing with misbehavior.

Try to grasp the meaning and purpose of the student's behavior. Is it a play for attention, power, revenge, or a display of inadequacy? Listen carefully, focusing on: (1) the beliefs the student is expressing, (2) the feelings she is experiencing, (3) the nonverbal messages she is sending through facial expressions, posture, and tone of voice. By actively listening and silently communicating the appropriate feeling "You are very angry. . . You feel it is unfair," the adult will help the student feel understood, thus dissipating resistance and conflict.

Pinpoint the real issue. To resolve the conflict, work toward increasing the student's awareness of the real issue. The real motive is usually to gain attention, to obtain power and control, to get even, or to be excused from functioning.

You might use a tentative hypothesis alluding to the purpose, "Could it be that . . . ?" "Is it possible that . . . ?" Then paraphrase the purpose, "You want to keep me busy with you?. . . to prove you are boss? . . . to attempt to get even? . . . to show that you are not capable so that you will be excused?" The student will become less defensive and tend to respond more honestly if the hypothesis is posed tentatively. If the hypothesis is incorrect, nothing is lost, since no direct accusations have been made.

Involve students in considering alternatives. Discuss alternative behaviors and positive, active, and constructive ways to achieve the goal. For example, "How else might you . . . ?" Students who seek power as their goal can be encouraged to use their powers to help others. They can also be encouraged to choose to cooperate.

Get a commitment to a specific course of action. Ask the student for a specific contract indicating approach, steps to take, and results. It is a good idea for the commitment to be put in writing. Students enjoy being able to make decisions and choices in the development of the contract. Once the commitment has been made, no excuses are accepted for a student's failure to act in line with the contract.

Should the student not behave as indicated in the contract, don't ask why. Ask only when she intends to do so, thus getting a recommitment to action. If the plan is not working, it is well to consider whether the problem is with the plan or with the student. Sometimes it is necessary for the student to reconstruct the plan.

Do not punish; use logical consequences. Let the student learn from experience. For example, if a student is inattentive as instructions are given, do not repeat the directive until you have given your attention and help to those who are cooperating. The inattentive student will be expected to finish the work within the stated time or use personal time to do the work.

As another example, the student who does not behave appropriately with others is not permitted to associate with them until he chooses to behave properly. Preventing students from taking part in an experience until they are ready to cooperate is a logical consequence of misbehavior if the educator conveys the message as a logical consequence.

When students are unwilling to stay in their seats, the teacher might give a choice of either standing or sitting. If a student chooses to stand, he can make another decision the next day about whether to continue standing or to sit in the seat.

Conclusion

Discipline is often ineffective because school personnel use authoritarian procedures, hoping to force students to comply with their demands. These methods seldom work. However, discipline can be a vital part of the educational process if we reorient our thinking toward guidance rather than control. The use of natural and logical consequences teaches students to meet the needs of the situation as well as personal responsibility.

Questions for Further Thought

1. What drawbacks have you found when disciplining students using reward and punishment?
2. Identify three examples of how you have or could use natural consequences in your classroom.
3. How can teachers turn logical consequences into punishment?
4. Is it possible for a teacher to be both firm and kind?
5. What are some techniques that you have found helpful in order to be more consistent with students?
6. How do you "separate the deed from the doer" when working with students?
7. Give an example from your teaching experience where you "refused either to fight or to give in."
8. How do you let all of the students involved in a problem share in the responsibility?
9. Why is it important for you to talk less and act more in your teaching?
10. What do you do when you cannot think of a logical consequence?
11. Specifically what are you doing in your classroom to teach "inner" control to your students?

Situations: Try to identify whether the following examples are logical consequences or punishment, and why.

1. Rick wrote almost unintelligibly. His sentences were incomplete and words were missing. The teacher hunted through each paper until she found a complete sentence. Then she

showed Rick the complete sentence, underlined it, and said, "That's a very good sentence." Incidence of complete sentences went up.

2. Situation: A girl in a kindergarten class kept knocking down block buildings made by other children in the class. Action: The teacher said: "That wasn't your building; you can't destroy other people's work. Now let me help you build one of your own, so you won't be bothering the others."

3. The children in Jimmy's class agreed that anyone who didn't finish his math in the period before P.E. would not be able to go to P.E. When this rule was made, the teacher asked each child if he thought this was a fair rule, and all agreed. The next day during math time, Jimmy talked and did not get his work done. He protested when he was told that he would not be able to go to P.E., but when reminded of the discussion the day before, he said nothing. For two more days, Jimmy didn't finish his math before P.E. no fuss was made over Jimmy; he simply was not allowed to come to P.E. On the third day, Jimmy had his work done on time, and from then on he went to P.E. at the same time as the rest of the class.

4. I announced to the class that their English assignments had to be completed before I would excuse them for lunch. They had thirty minutes to complete a twenty-minute job. When lunch time came, I asked the children to hand me their assignments as they left the room. Richie did not have his assignment done so he just sat in his seat looking at me. I didn't say anything but walked over to my desk where I sat down and opened my lunchbox. He sat and looked at me for his entire lunch period. When the afternoon bell rang, Richie said that I had made him miss lunch. I said I didn't say he couldn't eat; I said he must do his English first!

5. The newly repainted bathroom walls showed evidence of shoe marks belonging to two fifth grade boys. When questioned about the matter, the boys admitted to intentionally marking the walls with their shoes. Their discipline was to work for the janitor during recess.

6. Drexel had a habit of changing channels on the TV during the class "TV Time" without class consent. The teacher decided that if Drexel could not let the other people watch the program of the group's choice, he would have to find another TV or get

group consent. Without these two options available, Drexel was asked to leave the room if he did not want to watch the program that was on. (Asselin, Nelson, and Platt, 1975, pp. 112–113)

References

ASSELIN, C., T. NELSON, and J. M. PLATT, *Teacher Study Group Leader's Manual.* Chicago: Alfred Adler Institute, 1975.

DINKMEYER, D. and G. D. MCKAY. *Systematic Training for Effective Parenting.* Circle Pines, MN: American Guidance Service, 1976.

GALLUP, G. H. Seventh Annual Gallup Poll of Public Attitudes Toward Education. *Phi Delta Kappan,* December 1975, pp. 227–241.

Additional Resources

BARUTH, L. and D. ECKSTEIN. *The ABC's of Classroom Discipline.* Dubuque, IA: Kendall/Hunt, 1976.

CARLSON, J. *The Basics of Discipline.* CMTI Press, Coral Springs, FL: 1978.

DINKMEYER, D., G. MCKAY, and D. DINKMEYER JR. *Systematic Training for Effective Teaching.* Circle Pines, MN: American Guidance Service, 1980.

DREIKURS, R. *Psychology in the Classroom.* New York: Harper and Row, 1968.

DREIKURS, R., B. GRUNWALD, and F. PEPPER. *Maintaining Sanity in the Classroom,* 2nd ed. Harper and Row, 1982.

5

Why Do They Do What They Do?

Teachers need to understand why their students act as they do in order to help the students develop healthier behavior. Because students behave in similar ways, *but for different reasons,* each must be dealt with individually.

Some teachers are unsuccessful in dealing with classroom management and motivation problems because they do not understand why the student behaves as he does. Even the best theories and solutions do not work when we misunderstand the purpose of a student's behavior.

Teachers sometimes support the behavior they are trying to eliminate. For example, the teacher who tries to talk to a child who is misbehaving to seek attention, gives attention to that individual. The teacher who argues with the student who is misbehaving to seek power, demonstrates to the child just how important power is.

There is no bag of tricks that can provide teachers with

solutions to all the problems they may encounter. Thus, it is important for teachers to understand behavior.

We all want to belong, to count for something. We all want to feel significant—whether it be in the family, the classroom, the peer group, or the community. In order to find our place in life, we behave in ways to achieve this goal.

All behavior has a purpose and is directed toward the achievement of a goal. By using the A B C System of understanding human behavior that follows, it is possible to accurately and quickly identify the goal.

This procedure involves:

1. Observing what the individual does
2. Identifying what the teacher does and how he or she feels
3. Recording the consequences of the transaction, or how the student responds to what the teacher does

After observing several situations, a behavioral pattern will emerge, thus revealing the individual's goal.

All misbehavior is the result of a child's mistaken assumption about the way to find a place and gain status. Children misbehave to reach one of four basic goals:

Goal 1: Attention. The child believes "I am important only when people notice me or are in my service," or "I'm not outstanding but *at least* I will not be overlooked if I can obtain special attention, fuss, or service."

Goal 2: Power. "I count in life when people do just what I want," or "I may not be a winner but *at least* I can show people they cannot defeat me or stop me from doing what I want or make me do what they want."

Goal 3: Revenge. The discouraged child who seeks this goal believes, "I count or I'm special only when I hurt," or, "People do not care for me, but *at least* I can do things to strike back when I am hurt."

Goal 4: Inadequacy. The child who seeks this goal has given up on life and feels, "I do not count, why bother?" or, "I will not be able to measure up, but at least if I do nothing people will leave me alone."

Table 5 uses the ABC System as a framework to identify four goals of misbehavior.

The understanding and facilitation of healthy, productive behavior can be seen in Table 6.

Once we understand a student's goal, we have an opportunity to become more effective in dealing with his or her behavior. Modification programs have three fundamental aspects:

1. Removing unwanted and inappropriate goals and their corresponding behavior.
2. Encouraging and developing already existing healthy goals and behavior.
3. Initiating new behavioral responses and healthy goals.

Although many educators concentrate on eliminating existing negative behavior, greater gains can be made by developing appropriate goals and responses.

In dealing with human behavior, it is helpful to understand a series of principles. These may serve as guidelines when the "ABC's" become clouded with overly complex situations.

1. All behavior has a purpose and is goal-directed. Although we are often unaware of its purpose, our behavior is purposive. We are not pushed by causes but rather pulled by goals and our own dynamic striving. An individual's actions, displayed through his interactions with others, reveal the purpose of his behavior. The consequence then becomes the cause of behavior.

2. Behavior is best understood in terms of its unity or pattern. An individual responds to any stimuli as a total person with thoughts, actions, and feelings that are all part of a meaningful pattern. Therefore, in order to understand the individual, we must perceive the pattern and help him in relation to it. To be special, to control, to be right, to get even, to be served are examples of patterns that reflect the unity of the individual.

3. Each individual strives for significance. We work toward achieving self-selected goals that we believe will give us importance in life. This striving for significance is the motivating force behind human activity. While all individuals do not

Table 5
Chart of the ABC System

GOAL OF MISBEHAVIOR	"A"	"B"	"C"		What the child is saying	Some corrective measures
	What the child does	What the teacher or parents do and how they feel	What the child does as the consequence			
Attention	Active and passive activities that may appear constructive or destructive	Annoyed; wants to remind, coax; delighted with "good" child	Temporarily stops disturbing action when given attention		I only count when I am being noticed or served	Ignore; answer or do the unexpected; give attention at pleasant times
Power	Active and passive activities only; destructive in nature	Provoked; angry; generally wants power challenged; "I'll make him do it." "You can't get away with it."	Intensifies action when reprimanded. Child wants to win; be boss		I only count when I am dominating; when you do what I want you to	Extricate self; act; do not talk; be friendly; establish equality; redirect child's efforts into constructive channels
Revenge	More severe; active and passive activities	Hurt; mad; "How could he do this to me?"	Wants to get even; makes self disliked; intensifies action in a hurtful fashion		I can't be liked; I don't have power, but I'll count if I can hurt others as I feel hurt by life	Extricate self; win child over; maintain order with minimum restraint; avoid retaliation; take time and effort to help child
Inadequacy	Passive activities that defy involvement	Despair; "I give up"	No reprimand, therefore no reaction; feels there is no use in trying; passive		I can't do anything right, so I won't try to do anything at all; I am no good	Encouragement (may take long); faith in child's ability

By Jon Carlson, modified from Children's Mistaken Goals chart by Nancy Pearcy of Corvalis, Oregon.

Table 6
The Goals of Positive Behavior

CHILD'S BELIEF	GOAL	BEHAVIOR	HOW TO EN-COURAGE POSI-TIVE BEHAVIOR
I belong by contributing	Attention; involvement	Helps; volunteers	Let child know his or her contribution counts, and that you appreciate it.
I can decide and be responsible for my behavior.	Power; autonomy; responsibility for own behavior	Shows self-discipline; does own work; is resourceful	Encourage child's decision-making; let child experience both positive and negative outcomes; express confidence in the child.
I am interested in cooperating.	Justice; fairness	Returns kindness for hurt; ignores belittling comments	Let child know you appreciate her or his interest in cooperating.
I can decide to withdraw from conflict.	Withdrawal from conflict; refusal to fight; acceptance of others' opinions	Ignores provocations; withdraws from power contests to decide own behavior	Recognize child's effort to act maturely.

By Don Dinkmeyer and Gary McKay. *STEP Parents Handbook.* Circle Pines, MN

seek to be significant in the same way, we all strive for a sense of importance. The way in which an individual seeks significance reveals his self-concept.

4. All behavior has social meaning. We are social beings who want to find our place in the group. We want to *belong.* All of our problems are basically problems of interaction with others. The significance of behavior lies in terms of our social transactions and the subsequent consequences. Social striving is of primary importance.

5. The individual's beliefs determine behavior. We give meaning to life. Reality is as we perceive it. What happens to us is not as significant as how we feel about it. Heredity and environment are not as important as our interpretation of what they mean to us and how we decide to deal with them. Each individual has the creative capacity to interpret his experiences to fit his own life style. For example, the sun represents something very different to the farmer, the poet, the sunbather, the albino, the Inca, and the physicist.

6. Belonging is a basic need. An individual can only be actualized to the extent that he finds his place. When a person doubts he is accepted or feels he does not belong, he experiences anxieties and apprehension. In understanding the individual, it is helpful to identify the sources of his acceptance and identity.

7. The basic need is to actualize human potential. Human needs arrange themselves in a hierarchy. Maslow (1970) rates them, beginning with the most immediate: physiological, safety, belonging, love, self-esteem, and self-actualization. An individual must deal with his lower hierarchy needs before he can become a fully functioning person.

Consequences:
Cues to Understanding

The following steps are helpful in understanding behavior:

1. *Observation:* See what happens in the child-teacher-child transaction. Record carefully what the child does, the teacher's reaction, and the child's response.
2. *Consequences of behavior:* Record the end result of the transaction. What happens to each person? What are their final feelings and behavior?
3. *Identification:* Identify the goal of the behavior. What is the purpose of the behavior? What is the payoff?
4. *Modification:* Hypothesize possible solutions and take steps to correct the misbehavior.
5. *Record:* Keep daily records on the child's behavior.

Observation

Observe and record what happens during the interaction between the student and the teacher. Simply record what you see. Offer no subjective accounts of why the events are occurring.

Accurate observation can be facilitated through the use of anecdotes. Such anecdotes are like pieces in a jigsaw puzzle. When put together, the overall picture becomes clear.

Describe the setting of the specific transactions, including verbal as well as nonverbal cues. The records should indicate what the student does, how the teacher responds, and how the student reacts to the teacher.

Following is a set of anecdotal records on Bill:

December 2, 1975—10:10 A.M.

Bill was sitting at his desk during mathematics class while the teacher was talking to the other sixth-graders at the front of the room. The teacher turned to write a problem on the blackboard, and Bill began talking to his neighbor. The teacher turned around, looked directly at Bill and asked him to be quiet. She then turned around toward the blackboard, and Bill went back to talking.

December 2, 1975—11:50 A.M.

At the end of the physical education period, the teacher blew her whistle and announced that it was time to put the basketballs away and to line up to return to the classroom. Bill continued to shoot baskets. After all the children had lined up, the teacher asked Bill to put the basketball away. He slowly dribbled the ball to the supply room and emerged with a grin on his face.

December 3, 1975—1:45 P.M.

During mathematics class, the children were told that they were to do their homework. The could read library books when they were finished. The teacher wrote the assignment on the board. All the children except Bill began to work on the assignment. Bill read his library book. The teacher noticed this and asked him whether he had finished his assignment. He replied, with a big grin on his face, no. Bill then began to work on his assignment.

December 3, 1975—3:00 P.M.

The children were told that they could get into line for dismissal. They all rushed for a place in line except Bill, who slowly walked to the front of the line and stood.

Anecdotal records reveal the social dynamics of a situation. At this point, it appears that the goal of Bill's misbehavior is attention.

Because the significance of behavior lies in its consequences, it is essential to note and record the result of the transaction. Describe the feelings and behavior of both the teacher and the student. Interviews with the participants, as well as observations, offer important clues to understanding.

Identification

Identify the goal of the student's misbehavior by determining the purpose of the behavior. The goal will be attention, power, revenge, or a display of inadequacy.

To identify the goal of behavior:

. Determine the meaning of the transaction that is occurring between the participants.
2. Check your spontaneous reaction. If you feel annoyed, the goal is usually attention. If you feel personally challenged, the goal is more likely to be power. If you feel hurt and angry, the goal is usually revenge. If you give up, the goal is probably inadequacy.
3. Note the student's response to correction. If he merely desires attention, he will stop the behavior when attention is obtained. If the student is seeking power, controls will only bring more resistance.

Modification

Once we know the purpose of a student's misbehavior, we can consider ways of changing that behavior. Misbehavior does not develop quickly but rather over a period of time. Likewise, misbehavior does not disappear overnight. It is not surprising at first to see a sharp increase in the frequency of the misbehavior. Allow enough time for corrective measures to have an effect on the student.

Record

It is extremely important to keep records of behavior. Without records it is difficult to tell which procedures are effective. Daily anecdotal records of the student's behavior provide feedback as to whether the corrective measures are bringing about change.

An effective way of recording behavior is to note the frequency of the misbehavior each day and to graph the results. If after a reasonable period of time there has been no change, it would be wise to reevaluate the behavior. You may be treating the wrong goal.

The case of Bill demonstrates the method proposed here. First, data were collected about Bill through observation. The observer then considered the consequences of the interaction. How did the teacher feel? How did the child react to the teacher's behavior? In this case, the teacher felt annoyed. Bill reacted to her reprimand by stopping his misbehavior for the time being.

From our superficial analysis of this hypothetical case, it appears that Bill was striving for attention. Having tentatively identified the goal of Bill's misbehavior, we must formulate corrective procedures. We might suggest that the teacher ignore Bill when he misbehaves and give reinforcement in the form of attention when he behaves in a desirable manner.

The next step is to evaluate our new approach to determine if Bill's behavior is changing. If after a reasonable period of time this technique is not successful, we may have identified the wrong goal. In order to determine the true goal, we must repeat the process—make new observations, examine consequences of the behavior, identify the goal of the behavior, devise ways of changing the behavior, and record what happens.

This record procedure, which is easy to follow and effective, is appropriate for guidance workers, teachers, and parents.

The Healthy Individual

It is important for teachers to have a clear idea of the characteristics and behaviors they want their students to acquire. Most people know what they do not want their children to do (that is, swear, interrupt, smoke, pick their nose, chew their fingernails) but are unclear as to the positive qualities they would like the children to develop. Once a teacher has a clear idea of desired traits, these characteristics can be encouraged. Following are some traits of a mentally healthy individual:

1. Respects the rights of others
2. Is tolerant of others
3. Is interested in others
4. Cooperates with others
5. Encourages others
6. Is courageous
7. Has a true sense of his own worth
8. Has a feeling of belonging
9. Has socially acceptable goals
10. Puts forth genuine effort
11. Meets the needs of the situation
12. Is willing to share rather than being concerned with "How much can I get?"
13. Thinks of "we" rather than just "I" (Dewey, 1971, p. 68)

The elimination of negative behavior has dominated psychology since its inception. What we need today is an educational or preventative philosophy. Mental health and positive personality development can no longer be left to chance. Health must be developed in a deliberate manner. Only through training and motivating parents and teachers in this area can we develop mentally healthy children. Additional information on this subject can be found in the work of Herbert Otto, especially *Family Strengths and Their Utilization in Marriage and Family Counseling* (1972) and *The Use of Family Strength Concepts and Methods in Family Life Education* (1975), and John Gilmore's *The Productive Personality* (1975).

Understanding Human Personality Development

The personality or *life style* of an individual evolves from a combination of the following four components:

1. Family atmosphere and values
2. Sex roles

3. Family constellation
4. Methods of child-rearing

In this section, each of these components will be examined in terms of its influence on the child.

The family, especially the parents, have the most significant influence on the personality development of the child. The family is the arena in which love, trust, acceptance, and actualization are cultivated. The child's position in the family constellation and his relationship with siblings also exert a tremendous impact.

As a child grows up in a family, he or she begins to feel support or opposition—acceptance or nonacceptance. Sometimes parents make mistakes in the way they deal with raising their children—mistakes that retard the development of cooperation. Parents unwittingly discourage children.

Family atmosphere. The child's first exposure to life is within the family environment. It is here that the child is introduced to values, beliefs, and feelings. The child learns to communicate by observing relationships within the family. If he sees his parents fighting or using power to gain control, the child may adopt this behavior. On the other hand, children learn cooperation in families that emphasize working together for mutual interest. Whether the behavior be positive or negative, a child always chooses to act in a way that he feels will be most effective.

Because of exposure, children often develop interests similar to those of their parents. If a family is interested in outdoor sports and music, the child will probably adopt such interests.

The child's pattern of behavior is not necessarily a "carbon copy" of the family pattern. Although similar traits are often found among family members, each child is free to accept or reject as he chooses. The decision as to how a child interprets what he percieves lies in his creative power.

Children respond in different ways to the same experiences and influences. They do not merely react. They adopt an individual attitude, depending on the impressions they form in early childhood. The decisive factor for the development of personality is not the influence of environment, but the attitude toward the environment the child adopts.

Sex roles.   Sex roles also influence personality development. As parents model the male and female roles, children learn what it is like to be a man or a woman. This not only involves learning what the same sex does, but also what the opposite sex does. It is in the home that the child learns about intimacy and how to deal with the same and opposite sexes. The child interprets what he sees and accepts or rejects what he feels is or is not feasible.

Family constellation.   Each child has a unique position in the family structure. The ordinal position (that is, first born, middle, youngest, or only child) influences the development of certain characteristic attitudes and traits.

The oldest child usually strives to be number one in all areas because this is the way he has entered the world. Because he is an only child for awhile, he feels dethroned when another child enters the family structure. When he can no longer be number one, he may decide to give up completely. If he feels he can't be the best in a useful way, he may revert to being the worst, which for him is another way of being first.

The second-born child usually feels a need to compete with the first born. Some second children compensate for a feeling of inferiority by overtaking the first born. If competition between the two is strong, the second usually strives to become what the first is not. The second born often excels in areas different from his older sibling.

The middle child usually feels "squeezed out." These individuals may view life as unfair, full of injustice, and, as a consequence, they may give up. Middle children who choose to compete often become more successful than the two other siblings. They then overcome big rivals and become number one.

The youngest child sees himself as the baby. These children sometimes are spoiled and feel entitled to special attention. They like to get their own way and frequently go through life feeling inadequate. Sometimes they take on the characteristics of being the cutest or most charming.

Only children usually grow up in an adult world and become very mature at an early age. They often feel they can take adult roles and that they are very special. Only children want to be catered to and in some instances never really grow up. They often have difficulty developing feelings.

The position of the child in the family, the number of children in the family, and the sexual distribution in the family constellation are additional factors that influence personality development. Birth order is not the sole determining factor as to how the child develops. The way in which the child perceives his environment, along with his creative and intellectual capacity, also influences his development. More information on life style and personality can be found in Eckstein, Baruth, and Mahrer's *Life Style: What It Is and How to Do It* (1975).

The following principles will help teachers establish democratic child-management procedures.

1. The teacher should understand the child and the purpose of his behavior or misbehavior.
2. The relationship between teacher and child should always be one of mutual respect.
3. Teachers should be both firm and kind. Firmness indicates respect for oneself, and kindness shows respect for the child.
4. The child should be valued as he is. His assets and strengths should be discussed, valued, and emphasized. A teacher should spend more time encouraging than correcting. One positive statement a day is a good motto.
5. Teachers should have the courage to live with their own inadequacies. They should accept themselves as well as the child.
6. Teachers must act more and talk less. Natural and logical consequences that teach respect for order should replace reward and punishment.
7. If a poor or ineffectual relationship exists, parents must have the patience and take time to make corrective efforts. Developing human relationships that are mutually satisfying requires awareness, but it is worth the effort.

Teachers also have a major effect upon the student's life style and behavior. Through understanding students' goals, teachers can effectively stimulate growth and utilization of potential. Research indicates that people operate at about 15 percent of their potential ability. If anything close to this figure is correct, what is it that we are doing to restrict growth?

Questions on Behavior and Personality

These questions contain the major points necessary to understand behavior and personality.

Questions for Further Thought

1. Use the ABC system of understanding human behavior with one of your students.
2. See if you can identify students in your classroom who exhibit each of the four goals of misbehavior. Which goal is most common? Which goal do you have most trouble with?
3. Once you have identified the goal of misbehavior, how do you modify your approach to working with the student?
4. How do you use information on the family constellation in your teaching?
5. Pick out a difficult student and use the five-step process to understand his or her behavior.
6. What are the characteristics that you look for in a healthy student? What do you do to promote these characteristics?

Activities

1. Pick one student and analyze his or her behavior using the following steps:
   a. Describe what your student did.
   b. Describe your feelings and how you reacted.
   c. Describe the consequences or how the student responded to your reaction.
   d. What do you think is the goal of misbehavior?
   e. Did you notice any positive goals?
2. Johnny is consistently late to school. He disturbs the class, either by talking out of turn, chatting with a neighbor, or getting out of his seat. When the teacher corrects Johnny for his behavior, he glares at her and asks, "Why?" Johnny continues, "The

other kids do it, why can't I?" He goes on disrupting. One day, after trying to get Johnny to settle down, she shakes him and sets him in his seat.

   a. Johnny is displaying what mistaken goal? (1) Attention-getting (2) Power struggle (3) Revenge (4) Displaying inadequacy

3. Tom is in the fifth grade. One morning he entered class with his hat, coat, boots, and gloves on and joined the group for the opening class activity. The children are provided lockers and remove their clothing before class. He was asked to go to his locker and hang up his outer garments. For the next three days, he continued this behavior and each time was asked to go to his locker and did so.

   a. Tom is displaying what mistaken goal? (1) Attention-getting (2) Power struggle (3) Revenge (4) Displaying inadequacy

4. The children must put their outer garments on after school. Jane is very slow and hardly moves. Her teacher attempts to assist her, but Jane kicks, bites, and scratches the teacher.

   a. Jane is displaying what mistaken goal? (1) Attention-getting (2) Power struggle (3) Revenge (4) Displaying inadequacy

5. Johnny is repeating the second grade. His spelling is poor. Johnny sits in class the entire day. He causes no disturbance and never participates. If called upon, he often says, "I don't know." On the playground he stands and watches.

   a. Johnny is displaying what mistaken goal? (1) Attention-getting (2) Power struggle (3) Revenge (4) Displaying inadequacy

6. Bessie is a repeater in the third grade. Her learning rate is probably slow. In arithmetic, for instance, she might put down anything for an answer, or she might copy the problems but put down no answers at all. She seems afraid to recite.

   a. Bessie is displaying what mistaken goal? (1) Attention-getting (2) Power struggle (3) Revenge (4) Displaying inadequacy

7. Hal seldom prepares his assignments, takes little interest in class discussions, and is habitually truant. In school he is nervous, irritable, and disrespectful. During an examination, the teacher happens to look at him, and he immediately remarks, "What are you watching me for?"

Hal is displaying what mistaken goal? (1) Attention-getting (2) Power struggle (3) Revenge (4) Displaying inadequacy

8. Charles, age fifteen and a half, is a student in the seventh grade. Charles is uncooperative, wanders around the classroom at will, and speaks out when he wishes. Frequently, he ignores the teacher's request to return to his seat and work at assigned tasks. When he does mind, he does so swaggeringly and soon is up again.

    Charles is displaying what mistaken goal? (1) Attention-getting (2) Power struggle (3) Revenge (4) Displaying inadequacy

9. Earl, age eight, is doing good class work but has manifested destructiveness, particularly in his art work and seat work. One day he plainly refuses to do his seat work. He is talking to another boy while the teacher is talking to the class. The teacher moves his seat and continues. Earl says, "This is just where I want to sit."

    Earl is displaying what mistaken goal? (1) Attention-getting (2) Power struggle (3) Revenge (4) Displaying inadequacy

10. Gene, age five, is in a morning kindergarten class. He takes at least fifteen minutes to take off his coat and get his rug. Then he stands by the door, waiting for the teacher to notice him. When she does, he walks slowly into the room, almost as if he wants her to say, "Hurry up!" or help him sit down.

    Gene is displaying what mistaken goal? (1) Attention-getting (2) Power struggle (3) Revenge (4) Displaying inadequacy

11. Ralph, age ten and a half, in fourth grade, is working with words and pictures that were to be pasted on construction paper. Ralph brings one that has been passed to him and shows the teacher that it has come unpasted. He seems concerned and anxious for the teacher to do something about the matter. The teacher asks him what he is going to do about it. He goes to his seat, holds the two papers in his hands, and looks forlorn and helpless.

    Ralph is displaying what mistaken goal? (1) Attention-getting (2) Power struggle (3) Revenge (4) Displaying inadequacy

12. Peter, age ten, in fifth grade, is a natural leader, well liked by his classmates. He dislikes all subjects but loves to entertain. He refuses to take part in any activity he does not organize. He distracts the attention of all who sit near him. The teacher tries

talking to Peter, reasoning with him, and giving him special duties.

Peter is displaying what mistaken goal? (1) Attention-getting (2) Power struggle (3) Revenge (4) Displaying inadequacy

13. Tony, age seven, wants to correct everyone and refuses to do what he is asked. He wants to lead the group and makes frequent comments regarding what the class should do. If any teacher or classmates urges, commands, or corrects him, he tightens himself and tries to do the opposite of what they say.

Tony is displaying what mistaken goal? (1) Attention-getting (2) Power struggle (3) Revenge (4) Displaying inadequacy

14. Dick, age seven and a half, misses much of the class work. He follows school routine when he hears. Such things as his class being called, or instruction for seat work, have to be repeated often. He plays well with other children

Dick is displaying what mistaken goal? (1) Attention-getting (2) Power struggle (3) Revenge (4) Displaying inadequacy

15. Ken is an eight-year-old child in the third grade. He poses a problem by not being a part of his classroom group and is reluctant to join his group, even on the playground. He is extremely quiet. There is no life or sparkle such as one might expect of an eight-year-old. He could easily be forgotten in a large classroom. He sits in his seat like a statue with a bland and oblivious expression.

Ken is displaying what mistaken goal? (1) Attention-getting (2) Power struggle (3) Revenge (4) Displaying inadequacy

16. Margie, age twelve, is in the seventh grade. Last year everyone gave up trying to help her. She stole frequently, fought with the teachers and pupils, and failed all her classes. She started this year in her old pattern, stealing three times in two weeks and fighting constantly. She is a middle child.

Margie is displaying what mistaken goal? (1) Attention-getting (2) Power struggle (3) Revenge (4) Displaying inadequacy

---

References

ADLER, A. *Understanding Human Behavior*. New York: Fawcett, 1957.

DEWEY, E. "Understanding Children's Behavior." *Counseling Psychologist,* 1971, 3(2).

DINKMEYER, D. C. *Child Development: The Emerging Self.* Englewood Cliffs, NJ: Prentice-Hall, 1965.

DINKMEYER, D. and J. CARLSON. "Consequences—Cues to Understanding." *Elementary School Journal,* April 1973, pp. 399–404.

DINKMEYER, D. and J. CARLSON. *Consulting: Facilitating Human Potential and Change Processes.* Columbus: Charles Merrill, 1973b.

DINKMEYER, D. and G. MCKAY. *Raising a Responsible Child.* New York: Simon and Schuster, 1973.

DINKMEYER, D. and G. MCKAY. *Systematic Training for Effective Parenting.* Circle Pines, MN: American Guidance Service, 1976.

DREIKURS, R. *Fundamentals of Adlerian Psychology.* New York: Greenburg, 1950.

DREIKURS, R., B. GRUNWALD, and F. PEPPER. *Maintaining Sanity in the Classroom.* New York: Harper & Row, 1971.

ECKSTEIN, D., L. BARUTH, and D. MAHRER. *Life Style: What It is and How to Do It.* Chicago: Alfred Adler Institute, 1975.

GILMORE, J. V. *The Productive Personality.* San Francisco: Albion, 1974.

KELLEY, E. C. *Education for What Is Real.* New York: Harper & Row, 1947.

MASLOW, A. *Motivation and Personality,* 2nd ed. New York: Harper & Row, 1970.

OTTO, H. *Family Strengths and Their Utilization in Marriage and Family Counseling.* Beverly Hills, CA: Holistic Press, 1972.

OTTO, H. *The Use of Family Strength Concepts and Methods in Family Life Education.* Beverly Hills, CA: Holistic Press, 1975.

OTTO, H. A. *Exploration in Human Potentialities.* Springfield, IL: Charles C. Thomas, 1966.

6

Communication: Learning to Give and Take

Listening is a most important skill. Students as well as teachers want to be understood, cared about, noticed, remembered, and listened to. These are basic goals of each human being.

Do you really listen to your students? Do they listen to you? Are you genuinely interested in each other? Do you hear the problems, needs, and wants of your students?

Listening is a two-way street. Both parties must be involved. Few teachers are naturally good listeners, and seldom take the time to listen to what their students are really saying.

Teachers often lament, "They don't listen to me," thereby blaming students for the problem. Perhaps it would be helpful to examine the way the teacher models listening and communication. Because it is a two-way process, a change in one party will influence the other.

It's easy and safe to have superficial conversations with uninvolved people; but to many people such conversation is not satisfying. Unless you and your students communicate who you really are, you cannot have a meaningful relationship. The teacher who deeply influences a student is the one who is genuine and transparent rather than a godlike figure the students never get to know.

Among the most memorable times in our lives are moments when someone takes time to listen. Ideas are important to our students, and they want to share them with us. They want us to be interested in what they are saying. Showing students understanding and becoming involved with them is what makes them feel good about themselves.

Listening involves a decision to pay attention. We show students we really care about them by listening. Stay with the HERE and NOW instead of talking about another time or a different place. The past and future only exist in your mind *right now.*

Actions speak louder than words and often convey to students what we really mean. Nonverbal language is just as important as verbal communication. We communicate by tone of voice, eye contact, posture, and body movements. These nonverbal signals show that we are really listening, only pretending to listen, or not listening at all.

Because children believe what they are *shown* rather than *told,* nonverbal signals give us away. Students easily recognize when we are not listening. Although we may respond, our nonverbal behavior says we are a million miles away.

As a teacher, it is important to send positive nonverbal signs. Be alert, sit up straight, lean forward, maintain eye contact, and let your face show interest. A warm, soft tone of voice conveys acceptance and understanding. Strive for harmony in communication at the nonverbal as well as verbal levels, recognizing that students read *signs,* not *minds.*

Listening without judging is a special art. It is not necessary that you agree with the students, but merely that you understand their point of view. Many teachers have trouble remaining silent to hear the student out. But there is no way to listen when you are talking. Communication is a social event that enables people to interact with one another and work cooperatively. In order to teach effectively, one must not only speak, but also listen.

Listen to the feelings as well as the words. If you don't

understand, ask, "Is this what you mean?" Say, "It sounds like you're saying. . ." Though students may seem irrational, listen to them. If we were in their shoes, we would probably be the same way. When you can understand the student's point of view, you are well on the way to more effective teaching.

Communication Blocks

Because few teachers have learned good communication skills, they respond to students in ways that actually block communication. Ineffective responses are nonhelping and sometimes hurtful, for they destroy communication.

All communication blocks include the following:

1. They are a put down to the student in some way.
2. They are ineffective in helping the student solve problems or feel better.
3. They make the relationship worse by causing the student to close off from the teacher or to withdraw from further exploration.
4. They cause separation of student and teacher rather than closeness.

Following are some frequently used phrases that interfere with effective teaching. As you become aware of these, you will know what phrases to avoid.

1. Directing students to do something in such a manner that gives them little or no choice. The teacher who uses this form of communication does not pay attention to feelings or explain commands.

"Do your work."

"Close the door."

2. Warning students that if their behavior continues, certain consequences will occur.

"Quiet down, or I'll double your homework assignment."

"If you come late one more time, I'll give you an *F*."

3. Telling students something they ought to do.

"You should exercise every day."

"You should do your homework right after school."

4. Trying to influence students with facts, information, and logic.

"This picture is better because it has brighter colors."

5. Providing answers for the student's problems.

"I advise you to take French this semester."

6. Criticizing a student's behavior.

"You talk too fast."

7. Praising a student's behavior

"You laugh at the right times."

8. Analyzing a student's behavior and communicating that you have the behavior figured out. Although such a response may be accurate, it is rarely helpful.

"You must have been smoking pot because your eyes are watery."

9. Changing the subject or not discussing the problem presented by the student. Some teachers believe that if they can keep their students busy thinking about something else, there will be no problem.

"I know you have a problem with your parents, but let me tell you about my parents."

10. Trying to talk a student out of his or her behavior. Because some people are uncomfortable talking about anything unpleasant, they hide the problem under a bouquet of optimism.

"You shouldn't feel like that. Everything will be okay."

Effective Listening

When people send messages, they seldom clearly express their real feelings. A student might say, "I hate the science fair," but what he might be feeling is that his project may not be chosen a winner. If the teacher responds only to the words, the student's real message is missed, and the student is left feeling that the teacher doesn't understand.

Reflective listening is a response in which you merely reflect back to the student the feeling and the circumstances or reasons for the feeling. This is the most effective method of communication. Reflective listening is a special way of telling students you understand what they are feeling.

Observations indicate that less than one out of a thousand times will a feeling response be made in a typical classroom. When teachers use reflective listening skills, students know they have been heard and understood.

> Jim tells you he gave up going to a party last night to study for his geometry exam and then failed it. A reflective listening reply could be, "You feel disappointed, Jim, because you stayed home to study and then didn't get a good grade."

You reflect back his feeling—"You feel discouraged, angry, and disappointed." You then reflect back the reasons for the feeling—"because, although you stayed home to study, you didn't get a good grade."

Reflective listening is like being a mirror. You do not repeat the student's exact words but rather reflect back what the student implied and said. This requires empathy, because you listen for the feelings as well as the words. Ask yourself, "What else is the student saying? Am I hearing pleasant or unpleasant feelings?"

Thousands of students go to bed each night starving for a few moments of understanding. Each student who enters your life is worth the effort it takes to make him feel understood. Understanding facilitates growth. Not understanding or ignoring leads to criticism and rejection.

Reflective listening takes practice. You must go beyond the

words you hear to detect the feeling that may not even have been expressed in words but was clearly part of the response.

> Joanne tells you she wants to get a job after graduation. Her parents insist on her going to college. She says they won't even listen to her point of view.

Ask yourself what Joanne is feeling. Then say, "You are feeling pressure from your parents and some frustration because you may not be able to do what you want to do." If you are wrong, the student will correct you and help you to gain an accurate understanding of the situation.

As you train yourself in reflective listening, it is helpful to use this formula: "You feel (feeling word) because (content)." Once you become comfortable with this, you may want to vary the way you express yourself by using some of the following:

"Could it be that . . . ?"

"I wonder if . . ."

"Correct me if I'm wrong, but . . ."

"As I hear it, you . . ."

"What I hear you saying is . . ."

Choose your "feeling" word carefully, being sensitive to the way you think a student will respond to a certain word. Be careful not to underestimate the intensity of a student's feelings.

It takes practice for us to become aware of our feelings. We are used to hiding or ignoring how we feel. Many people do not have a very large vocabulary of feeling words. We may say we are angry when in reality we may be frightened, hurt, uncomfortable, or sad. As you expand your feeling word vocabulary you will be better able to respond accurately and sensitively to your students.

Following is a list of pleasant and unpleasant feeling words. Add your own words to the list:

WORDS EXPRESSING POSITIVE FEELINGS

Accepted	Appreciated	Calm	Comfortable
Adequate	Befriended	Capable	Compassionate
Affectionate	Brave	Cheerful	Confident

Content	Free	Interested	Respected
Courageous	Fulfilled	Joyful	Safe
Delighted	Generous	Kind	Satisfied
Determined	Glad	Loved	Secure
Ecstatic	Grateful	Loving	Super
Elated	Great	Peaceful	Surprised
Encouraged	Happy	Pleased	Sympathetic
Energetic	Helpful	Proud	Terrific
Excited	High	Refreshed	Thrilled
Exuberant	Important	Relaxed	Trusted
Fascinated	Inspired	Relieved	Valued

WORDS EXPRESSING NEGATIVE FEELINGS

Abandoned	Defeated	Insecure	Rejected
Afraid	Different	Insignificant	Restless
Alone	Disappointed	Intimidated	Scared
Ambivalent	Discouraged	Irritated	Shocked
Angry	Dominated	Isolated	Skeptical
Annoyed	Dubious	Jealous	Squeezed
Anxious	Embarrassed	Left out	Startled
Apprehensive	Empty	Lonely	Surprised
Awful	Envious	Mad	Tense
Bad	Exhausted	Melancholy	Tired
Betrayed	Fearful	Miserable	Threatened
Bitter	Foolish	Mixed-up	Trapped
Bored	Frightened	Nervous	Troubled
Bugged	Frustrated	Overwhelmed	Unappreciated
Burdened	Grief	Pushy	Uncomfortable
Caught between	Guilty	Put down	Uneasy
Cheated	Helpless	Pain	Unloved
Confused	Hurt	Persecuted	Unsettled
Crushed	Incapable	Pressured	Uptight

Open and Closed Responses

Once students realize that you really care about them, it is important to encourage them to continue to share their feelings so that you can help them. This can be done by learning to make *open* rather than *closed* responses.

When our response reflects the feelings and the circumstances of those feelings accurately, we are making an open response. Closed responses include our interpretations and judgments, and consequently tend to stop communication.

Closed responses may understate or not even acknowledge the student's feelings.

> Jenny says, "I wish we didn't have to wear uniforms. Patty doesn't have to wear them at her school."

A closed response might be:

> "That's the rule, and there is a good reason for it."
>
> or
>
> "You just want to show off all your clothes. A lot of students don't have as much to wear as you do."

An open response could be:

> "I'm sensing that you think it's not fair to have to wear uniforms when your friends do not have to wear them."

Problem Ownership

Reflective listening is the first step in helping students solve their problems. However, this really doesn't help when the teacher has a problem. The solution to this situation is an I-message, in which the teacher shares how he or she feels with the student.

It is necessary to distinguish between problems that students have that cause *them* a problem, but not the teacher, and those that have a direct effect on the teacher by interfering with his needs, rights, or safety.

Failure to understand who owns the problem and to act accordingly is a serious block to a healthy relationship. Problem ownership is important because teachers must handle situations differently when a student owns the problem than when the teacher owns the problem.

To determine ownership, ask yourself, "Does this problem directly interfere with my teaching, my rights, or my safety? Am I feeling angry, frustrated, or upset because of this behavior?" If so, then the teacher owns the problem; it is his responsibility.

If Paul draws pictures all over the pages of his social studies book and you are responsible for the books in your classroom, then you own the problem.

On the other hand, if Judy spends a lot of time daydreaming when you are trying to teach English grammar, then the problem belongs to Judy. Her daydreaming does not tangibly or concretely interfere with your teaching activities.

If David tells his teacher that he is angry because his parents won't let him go to the rock concert, then the student owns the problem. David's anger does not tangibly affect the teacher. It does affect the student; the problem belongs to David.

No matter how effective you are as a teacher, students will always have their own unresolved problems. And there will always be students who behave in ways that interfere with your needs and desires. It is crucially important to respond effectively.

When problems belong to the whole class, it is best that the entire group experience the consequences of the behavior. If the class is noisy and out of line before dismissal, then the whole group may need to stay after school to discuss where their responsibilities lie.

You- and I-Messages

When the problem belongs to the teacher, s/he usually wants the students to listen to how s/he feels. This is the time to use an I-message, in which you state your concerns and feelings in a quiet, respectful manner. For example, "Phil, when you don't learn your lines in the play, I feel frustrated because opening night is this weekend, and I want to have a professional performance."

Too often we use you-messages, which criticize and blame, such as, "Phil, you're holding up the whole cast because you don't know your lines. You're ruining the show." You-messages embarrass, hurt, and put down the student. Rather than inviting cooperation, they provoke hostile, defensive behavior. They reinforce misbehavior.

You-messages become self-fulfilling prophecies. When you

continually tell someone, "You never do anything right," the person begins to believe it, and the accusation becomes reality.

Although our intent may be to motivate, a you-message usually doesn't work. If we say, "Mandy, you're not going to pass biology if you don't finish your lab work," Mandy may become hostile and defensive, or she may refuse to accept the blame dished out in the you-message.

On the other hand, an I-message allows a teacher who is affected by the behavior of a student to express the effect it has on him or her and at the same time leaves the responsibility for modifying the behavior to the student. For example, "Mandy, when you don't finish your lab work, I feel frustrated because I'm trying to help you do well in this biology class."

I-Messages

I-messages promote cooperation rather than anger and resentment. When you express yourself in an I-message, you assume responsibility for your own feelings and leave the students' behavior up to them. For example, "I'm frustrated when you don't pay attention because it is necessary to understand this problem before we move on to the next chapter."

I-messages tell the students you have confidence that they will help out with the problem. You give them the opportunity to choose to cooperate. You might say, "Bill, when you act like a clown in class, I feel angry because the students pay attention to you and not me, and I am unable to teach the lesson."

It takes a lot of courage to confront a student directly with an I-message. Exposing your feelings to the students is a risk. It's easier to hide your feelings and blame the students. It's safer to have superficial relationships, play games, and act out roles.

Most teachers are comfortable lecturing, probing, directing, and evaluating. Revealing inner feelings and needs is scary, but once you open up yourself, the students will see you as a real human being just like themselves. As the students realize that teachers, too, have feelings, you will have a much greater chance of influencing them in a positive way. Once they know that you can feel hurt, disappointment, fear, and frustration, the students will see you as a genuine person with whom they can have a meaningful relationship.

Angry I-Messages

It is important that I-messages be communicated calmly and in a nonjudgmental manner. An I-message stated in an angry, critical tone is really just a disguised you-message.

Anger is often used to control, get even, win, or cover up fear and embarrassment. However, attacking students does not create an encouraging atmosphere in the classroom. A student who is spoken to in anger does not feel like cooperating.

Anger is usually mixed with other feelings like worry, concern, and anxiety. Teachers can learn to express the other feelings—the ones that tell the students you care about them. I-messages can show these positive feelings and consequently result in cooperation and thoughtfulness from the students. For example, "Erin, when you don't return from recess, I get concerned about your safety because I care about you." This I-message conveys concern and caring. When you feel angry, it is important to separate your hostile feelings from those of concern.

Putting an I-Message Together

I-messages focus on feelings and behavior rather than on individuals. They separate the deed from the doer. The teacher's feelings and the student's behavior are the focus. I-messages connect the teacher's feelings with the consequence of the student's behavior. I-messages begin with "when."

"When I see the equipment left out . . ."

"When you forget your homework . . ."

"When the class is noisy . . ."

The I-message does not attack the person but merely describes a behavior.

The real reason for the concern is usually not the behavior, but rather the consequences of the action. Thus, I-messages use the word "because" to connect the teacher's feelings with the consequence of the student's behavior that upsets the teacher.

The formula is: When _____, I feel _____ because _____."

"When I keep getting interrupted, I feel irritated because I'm trying to finish this chapter before the bell rings."

I-messages do not have to follow the three-part formula. At times the feeling statement can even be eliminated. For example:

"I can't teach when it's so noisy in the classroom."

"I can't give you a grade on your report card when you don't hand in your assignments."

Sometimes the word "you" is part of an I-message. As long as the "you" does not convey criticism or blame, it is still an I-message.

"Susan, when you chew gum during class, I feel irritated because that violates a school rule."

I-messages focus on the teacher rather than on the student. I-messages are not critical or blaming statements. They stress the consequences of the behavior rather than the behavior itself. I-messages are valuable forms of communication in the classroom.

It takes time for students to get used to I-messages. Often they seem surprised to discover how their teachers feel. Students seldom realize how their behavior affects others, but once they understand, they usually respond in a more cooperative, thoughtful way.

Although I-messages are especially effective in dealing with misbehavior, they also can provide healthy encouragement when used with positive behavior. For example:

"Terry, I appreciate your helping Chris with his math. That gives me time to finish the lesson with the rest of the class."

"Beth, thanks for sorting those papers. Your help means a lot to me."

Open vs. Closed Questions

Problem solving is an important part of communication. As you address the particular problem, you can encourage creative thinking on the part of the student by the way you phrase your questions.

There are two ways to ask a question. An *open* question does not accuse or criticize the student and encourages further discussion. A *closed* question tends to blame the student and stop communication.

Open questions, which allow a wide variety of responses, usually begin with *who, what, when, where, which,* or *how.* Closed questions usually call for a yes or no answer and begin with a verb or *why.*

Some closed questions might be:

"Don't you think this is a better way?"

"Are you just going to sit there and look at me?"

"Why are you so impatient?"

"Aren't you finished yet?"

Examples of open questions include:

"How are you doing with the chapter on the Constitution?"

"What concerns you about that relationship?"

"What does Mike do that irritates you?"

When you are looking for a yes or no answer, closed questions are appropriate.

"Do you understand the answer now?"

"Would you like a few more minutes to finish?"

If a student answers an open question with "fine," "terrible," or "nothing," you might ask:

"What do you mean by 'terrible'?"

"Tell me more about it."

"Could it be that . . . ?"

Teachers can use a "why" question in a nonjudgmental way by phrasing it carefully, such as, "Do you have any ideas about why that may have happened?" This also gives the students a chance to think about the purpose of their actions.

Types of Requests

Requests can be classified into four categories based on what the student is seeking (Gazda et al, 1976). These include:

> Request for action
> Request for information
> Request for understanding involvement
> Request for inappropriate interaction

For each of these requests, there is an effective response.

Request for action. The most common request is one for action. A student may ask, "May I borrow your book?" The only response necessary is something simple such as, "Yes, you may. Here it is."

Sometimes the request is not so straightforward, and the meaning may only be inferred from the student's statement. The student may say, "I wish I had not left my book at home. Now I'll have to guess at the assignment." In such a case, the student could be thinking, "I would like to borrow your book, but I'm afraid you might not let me use it." Thus, the student states his or her need and waits for the teacher to respond.

Requests for action sometimes appear simple but actually require additional information and understanding of the conditions before an appropriate response can be made. An example of this is a request for more time to complete an assignment. The teacher must consider whether or not fulfilling the request is in the best interest of the student. Helping sometimes means doing and sometimes means not doing what is requested by the student.

Request for information. A request for information is similar in dynamics to a request for action. A student may ask, "Must I take two years of a language to be able to go to college?" The straightfoward answer could be: "Yes," "No," "I don't know," or, "It depends on the college."

Often a request for information is implicit, such as, "I wonder how many years of language you must have to go to college." Although what is implied is open to speculation, the teacher would again respond in a direct manner. If the student does not pursue the interaction, you can assume that the request for information has been adequately fulfilled. Should the student continue the transaction, it may lead to the development of a request for understanding/involvement.

Request for understanding/involvement. A request for understanding/involvement focuses on the student's need to be understood and to become involved in a helping relationship. The student is asking the teacher to respond to his or her feelings.

The request may be explicit such as: "Will you please help me find a way to convince my parents that all kids don't need to go to college?" Or it may be implicit as, "I don't understand why my parents think that everyone should go to college."

In both cases, the student is asking for understanding and involvement. The student wants empathy, warmth, and respect. It takes very special skills to deal effectively in such personally meaningful and sensitive areas.

Teachers must be sensitive to statements that *appear* to be simple requests for action or information but are really requests for understanding. Because some students have trouble asking for help directly. they might say, "I wonder why *some parents* feel that everyone must go to college." What the student really might be asking is, "How can I convince *my parents* that I should be able to choose to work rather than attend college?"

As you become sensitive to the needs of the students, you will be able to detect requests for understanding/involvement no matter how disguised they might be.

Requests for inappropriate interaction. There are certain interactions that are potentially damaging. These include: gossiping, griping excessively, spreading rumors, soliciting a dependency relationship, and encouraging activities that are counter to the benefit of others.

In an attempt to draw the teacher into gossip, a student may say, "I heard that our football coach is going to be fired. Isn't that awful?"

For the teacher to offer an opinion or to speculate on the information would be unhealthy. Rejection of the statement could convey rejection of the student and consequently discourage further requests for understanding/involvement relationships.

Perhaps the most effective way to handle the situation would be to let the student know you do not want to become involved in that kind of interaction by saying, "Since I'm not aware of the situation, I don't feel that I have a right to comment on it." Although this reply tells the student that you heard what was said and do not want to become involved, it still keeps the lines of communication open. Furthermore, it gives the student a positive response model should she become engaged in inappropriate interactions.

There is a definite risk involved in responding to a request for inappropriate interaction. It is important to not embarrass the student for fear that he or she might avoid an understanding/involvement relationship in the future. However, silence also presents a risk in that it may convey consent. Because of their silence, teachers sometimes lose an opportunity to help.

Summary

Communication means a decision to pay attention. Through sensitive listening, teachers can build healthy relationships with their students. Because few people are naturally good listeners, effective communication skills must be learned.

Own your feelings. Acknowledge responsibility for what you are saying, feeling, and doing. Risk saying what *you* feel, telling your students what *you* want, sharing where *you're* at.

Do not assume that you and your students speak the same language, even when you and they use the same words. Check that you understand the students as they wish to be understood. Analyzing and interpreting are not the same as understanding.

Say what you mean. Be sure that your words, the way you act, and your feelings all match. Once you acquire healthy communication tools, you will be a more effective teacher.

Questions for Further Thought

1. How can teachers be better listeners?
2. How can listening for feelings create a better relationship with students?
3. Why are open responses more effective than closed responses?
4. What is the purpose of reflective listening?
5. How does body language affect our communication with students?
6. Why is it important to determine who owns the problem in the classroom?
7. When do you find it useful to use I-messages with your students?
8. Practice talking with your students for one entire class period without using the word "you."
9. Why do you-messages often fail to motivate?
10. Demonstrate both an open and closed question that you could use in a current lesson.

Exercises

Reflective listening

Following are a number of statements made by students. Determine responses that address the feelings as well as the words.

"My parents won't let me go to Mary's party. They think I'll get in trouble."

"My report card was terrible. I'm grounded for the rest of the semester; now I can't even use the car."

"I try so hard to be good in art, but I get embarrassed because I can't draw anything."

"I really hate this school. It's just like a prison. I wish I could transfer."

I-Messages

Write an I-message in response to the following situations.
1. You are teaching a class. Two students keep passing notes back and forth.
2. Peter is a very bright student. However, he uses his creativity to bring humor to the classroom while you're trying to teach social studies.
3. You agreed to stay after school to help a student. You've waited fifteen minutes and the student has not shown up. You have to leave because you are expecting company for dinner.
4. One of your students has been changing gradually. He has been arriving late to class and sometimes does not come at all.

Open and closed responses

List two open and two closed responses for each of the following statements made by students.

"I never have enough time to do my homework."

"I don't know why we have to do math problems every night."

"My English teacher makes me so upset that I don't want to go to that class anymore."

"I'm so tired of getting up in the morning and going to school."

"I'm really having a difficult time getting my parents to trust me."

References

DINKMEYER, D., G. D. MCKAY, and D. DINKMEYER, JR. *Systematic Training for Effective Teaching.* Circle Pines, MI: American Guidance Service, 1980.

EGAN, G. *The Skilled Helper.* Monterey, CA: Brooks/Cole, 1982.

GAZDA, G. M. and others. *Human Relations Development: A Manual for Educators,* 2nd ed. Boston: Allyn and Bacon, 1976.

GORDON, T. *Teacher Effectiveness Training.* New York: Peter H. Wyden, 1974.

103

GRAY, D., and J. TINDALL. *Peer Power.* Muncie, IN: Accelerated Development, 1978.

MYRICK, R., and T. ERNEY. *Youth Helping Youth: A Handbook for Training Peer Facilitators.* Minneapolis: Educational Media Corporation, 1979.

Additional Resources

CARKHUFF, R. R., D. H. BERENSON, and R. M. PIERCE. *The Skills of Teaching: Interpersonal Skills.* Amherst, MA: Human Resources Development Press, 1977.

WITTMER, J., and R. MYRICK. *Facilitative Teaching.* Pacific Palisades, CA: Goodyear Publishing Co., 1974.

7

Growing Through Problems

Jack, a sophomore in high school, is often absent from class. Sarah, a thirteen-year-old, stares out into space daydreaming instead of listening to the mathematics lesson. Darren, a first-grader, cries several times each day. Martha, a sixth-grader, refuses to play games with the other students and just stands on the sidelines watching. Peter, a third-grader, wanders around the classroom disturbing other students. Dick, a ninth-grader, seems to thrive on arguing and debating with almost everything his peers say. Danny, quarterback of the varsity football team, quits the team without any explanation.

These and many other behaviors are clues from students indicating that something is wrong. These behaviors are messages saying that the students are having problems. Such difficulties tend to block the capacity for formal learning. Problem solving is an essential skill for effective teaching and human functioning.

Problems and problem solving are bridges to meaningful

learning. In the process of solving problems, learning occurs. When teachers and professors provide students with mountains of information about problems the students do not have, or perhaps ever will, the educators operate in direct contradiction to this principle.

Problems must precede answers. This is why advice is seldom really helpful to other people. Advice is usually avoided in the modern practice of counseling, psychiatry, and social work. Teachers are most helpful when they encourage active searching for answers to problems. The process of searching for meaning may be far more important for the growth of the individual than the answers he or she discovers.

The chapter on communication provided effective listening skills. As students clarify their thoughts and feelings, they are able to deal with problems more effectively. Students can often resolve their own problems simply by being heard by an understanding teacher. The answer or solution may occur during the dialogue with the teacher or at a later time.

> *Student:* This school sure isn't as good as my last one. The kids there were friendly.
> *Teacher:* You feel pretty left out here.
> *Student:* I sure do. I feel left way out. The kids won't even play with me at recess.
> *Teacher:* You feel really dejected because you try to play with the kids, and they won't respond.
> *Student:* Well, maybe I haven't tried. I guess I just figured that it's up to them to ask me to play. Isn't that the right way?
> *Teacher:* You feel confused about whether to approach the other students or not.
> *Student:* Well, yes . . . but I guess I know that I need to make the first move. As a matter of fact, I think I'll try to get into the game they always play after lunch.

There are, of course, times when students need help in exploring alternative solutions to their problems. Effective teachers help students to consider alternatives and choose pathways that make sense to the students.

This process of solving problem or exploring alternatives should not be confused with giving advice. Offering advice such as, "If I were you . . . ," "The thing for you to do is . . . ," or, "Do this . . . ," is not effective because advice does not help students learn how to solve their own problems. Advice gives the student the opportunity to become dependent upon the teacher, thus avoiding responsibility. If the advice doesn't work, the student holds the teacher responsible. The feeling of, "I need to turn to 'authorities' when stress occurs," may prevail. Many students resist taking advice. They either doubt that the advice will work because they think the teacher *really* doesn't understand, or they don't want to do what the teacher says. Advising implies superiority on the part of the teacher and indicates to the student that the teacher doesn't believe the student can solve his own problems. Students, especially adolescents, spend much time reacting to this attitude.

Educators can best help students by assisting them in identifying and evaluating alternative solutions to their problems. By helping the student evaluate each pathway, he or she is better able to choose a healthy solution.

When teachers function in this fashion, the following benefits usually result:

1. Strong and angry feelings of students are dealt with and defused.
2. Students learn not to be afraid of feelings and problems.
3. Problem solving influences other aspects of the student's life.
4. Students learn to accept *responsibility* for analyzing and solving problems.
5. Students develop more respect for themselves and their teachers; this results in students who listen and classrooms where learning thrives.
6. A closer, more meaningful relationship develops between teacher and student.

Six Steps of Problem Solving

Teachers are required not only to solve problems, but also to teach students problem-solving techniques. Many educators do not know what to do when problems arise other than to try a variety of tactics to avoid them. Avoidance usually does not solve the problem. The skills of problem solving can be learned as we examine the following Six Steps of Problem Solving.

1. Clearly understand the problem through active listening.
2. Identify possible solutions through brainstorming.

3. Assist the student in making a decision.
4. Discuss the results of the decision.
5. Determine how to implement the decision and obtain a commitment.
6. Develop criteria for success and a time for evaluation.

Clearly understand the problem through active listening.
Once teachers understand the problem, they have made a giant step toward its solution. Defining a workable problem is the most difficult step in problem solving. The process of active listening helps us clearly to understand the difficulty. It is important to define the problem in terms of needs rather than solutions. The following are statements of needs or unmet needs:

"I don't like to repeat the spelling tests."

"I can't hear the group I'm working with."

A message such as "I want the room quiet" gives the solution the student wants but does not express needs. The following example shows how the problem can be understood through active listening.

> *Larry (crying):* I'm not gonna play with them anymore. I hate them.
> *Teacher:* Sounds like you are really angry with the gang.
> *Larry:* Yeah, every day when I want to play with them we argue and a fight breaks out. And the problem is that they think it's all my fault.
> *Teacher:* You're feeling hurt about being left out and not being understood.
> *Larry:* Yeah, I really hate being left out of the gang.

In order to be a successful, active listener, the teacher must believe that students can solve their own problems. Because students often do not find solutions quickly, educators must have patience, remembering that the purpose of active listening is to facilitate solution finding—a process that may take days, weeks, or even months.

The teacher must genuinely accept the student's feelings. This does not mean accepting feelings the teacher thinks the student "should" have. By providing an atmosphere in which feelings can be openly expressed, examined, and explored, students have an opportunity to free themselves of troublesome feelings.

The teacher must understand that feelings are often quite transitory. They exist only as of the moment. Active listening helps students move from momentary feeling to momentary feeling. Thus, feelings get defused, dissipated, and released. "This, too, shall pass" applies to most human feelings.

The teacher must want to help students with their problems and must make time to do this.

Teachers must experience the students' feelings as if they were their own, but not let the feelings of the students become their own. Although empathy is essential, separateness must be maintained.

The problem that the student initially presents is usually not the real problem. Through active listening the student is able to clarify the real issue. Some educators are uncomfortable with real-life, "gutty" problems. In such a case, it is important for the teacher to channel the student to someone who is more skilled in dealing with the real-life problems that students so often experience.

Teachers must respect the confidential nature of whatever the student reveals. Nothing will destroy the teacher-student relationship more quickly than gossiping and openly discussing the student's problems with other teachers.

Identify possible solutions through brainstorming. Once the problem has been accurately defined, both teacher and student can begin identifying possible solutions. It is wise for teachers to hear students' ideas before offering their own. If the teacher makes too many suggestions, the student may become too dependent on the educator's ideas rather than his or her own.

Because of inexperience, sometimes a student cannot generate realistic ideas. In such a case, suggestions can be offered in a tentative form: "Have you considered what might happen if you . . . ?" "Have you thought about . . . ?" Have the student record the various solutions. Do not require justification or documentation of ideas.

Do not evaluate any solutions. There are no wrong answers in brainstorming. Be crazy! Be silly! Encourage different and unique solutions. Evaluation comes with the next step. If it occurs at this stage, the student might feel judged and possibly stop volunteering ideas.

Facilitate participation through using open-ended statements such as, "What are some of the possible solutions to this problem?" "There are no right answers. Let's see how many ideas we can come up with." Accept all ideas. The goal at this step is *quantity,* not quality.

The example that follows shows how possible solutions can be generated through brainstorming.

> *Teacher:* Would you like to think of some ways that you could solve this problem?
> *Larry (still upset):* Like what?
> *Teacher:* What do you want to happen?
> *Larry:* I don't want to argue and fight with the gang anymore.
> *Teacher:* What are some things you could do instead?
> *Larry:* I don't know.
> *Teacher:* I realize that you are not sure, but what are some of the possibilities?
> *Larry:* Keep quiet when I'm near them.
> *Teacher:* Any other ideas?
> *Larry:* I could keep talking but watch what I say. (pause) I could go to the guys and announce that I don't want to fight and argue, and I could ask for their help.
> *Teacher:* Yes, anything else?
> *Larry:* I could try to build the other guys up when they do good . . . I usually just make wisecracks when they fail . . . I could begin to invite different guys over to my house after school. . . .

Assist the student in making a decision.   Once alternative solutions have been listed, the teacher can help the student evaluate the various possible solutions. Again, it is the student's responsibility to choose and the teacher's responsibility to facilitate the process. Questions such as, "Which idea do you like the best?" and "Which alternative would you like to do?" are helpful in directing discussion. In the example with Larry and the teacher this step might be as follows:

> *Teacher:* Gee, Larry, you have thought of many good alternatives.
> *Larry (surprised):* I didn't realize that there were that many.
> *Teacher:* Which one do you think is the best one?

> *Larry:* I think I ought to go to the guys and honestly tell them that I don't want to argue and fight anymore, and I'll ask for their help.

Even though there were many good alternatives, Larry chose the one that was best for him. When someone believes an idea or solution is best, he or she usually makes it happen, as in the "self-fulfilling prophecy."

Discuss the results of the decision. It is helpful to have the student consider the possible outcome of his or her decision. If a student does not think through the choices, the student may discover he has chosen a short-range solution to a long-range problem. In our example, the fourth step would be illustrated as follows:

> *Teacher:* Why did you choose that idea?
> *Larry:* Because I know the guys are really mad, and I don't even think they would give me a chance if I didn't.
> *Teacher:* Just what exactly are you going to say?
> *Larry:* Well, let's see. (pause) "Hey, guys, I want to tell you something. I'm sorry for the way I've been acting, and I really want to play without arguing or fighting. I'd like to be able to start again with a clean slate and hope that each of you will help me."
> *Teacher:* All right, I like that! What do you think they'll say?
> *Larry:* I know they'll say okay.
> *Teacher:* Then what will you do?
> *Larry:* Ask them which team I'll be on and work hard playing ball and not arguing.
> *Teacher:* Can you foresee any problems with this alternative?
> *Larry:* Yeah, it's gonna be hard work for me to act differently, but it'll be worth it.

The teacher and student should discuss all the possible things that might go wrong and how they would deal with each situation.

Determine how to implement the decision and obtain a commitment. Many potentially productive problem-solving efforts end in frustration because decisions are not implemented. Teachers often take it for granted that the student knows what to do, how to do it, and when to begin. A good way to encourage implementation and ensure that the student knows what to do is through obtaining a commitment from the student. To get a commitment, ask, "What have you decided to do?" and "When are you going to do this?"

> *Teacher:* Larry, have you decided that this is what you want to do?
> *Larry:* Yes.
> *Teacher:* When are you going to do it?
> *Larry:* I was going to do it today after lunch, but I think I'll let things cool down a little and do it before lunch tomorrow.

Develop a criterion for success and a time for evaluation. Evaluation is necessary in order to check out the effectiveness of the efforts. The teacher needs to help the student develop a criterion for success and plan a time for evaluation. If the solution does not work, begin the six-step method again.

> *Teacher:* How will you know if your plan is working?
> *Larry:* I guess if I can play with the guys and not argue or fight.
> *Teacher:* Okay. I'd like you to give the idea a chance to work. How about giving the idea a good test, and then we can talk again next week at this time and see how it's going. Are you willing to do that?
> *Larry:* Sure—thank you!

The teacher is firm but kind with Larry, showing concern for him by scheduling another meeting. Statements like "How will you do this?" and "When shall we discuss this again?" are helpful to the student during this step.

Problem Ownership

It is essential to determine who owns the problem. The techniques of reflective listening and exploring alternatives are especially helpful when the student is experiencing the problem. Remember, to determine problem ownership, simply ask Whose problem is it? Who is experiencing difficulty with whom? Whose purposes are not being met?

The following points clearly illustrate problem ownership:

1. If the student has a problem because he is thwarted in satisfying a need, it is not the teacher's problem, because the student's behavior in no way interferes with the teacher. Consequently, the student owns the problem.

2. If the student is satisfying his own needs, is not thwarted, and his own behavior is not interfering with the teacher, there is no problem in the relationship.

3. If the student is satisfying his own needs and is not thwarted, but his behavior is a problem to the teacher because it is interfering, the teacher owns the problem.

A practical rule of thumb on problem ownership is that when a student comes to you with a problem, the student owns the problem; and when the teacher sees or hears something he or she cannot accept, the teacher owns the problem.

Teachers behave quite differently when students own problems than when the teachers own them. Thus, it is vital for teachers to be able to distinguish between those problems students have that cause the student a problem, but not the teacher, and those that have a direct effect on the teacher by interfering with the needs of the teacher.

The following procedure is useful when there is a problem in your relationship with a student (or any other person), and/or when you become aware that someone else is feeling upset.

1. What is the problem? Briefly state the problem without placing blame on anyone. Talk about your feelings in relation to the problem.
2. Who owns the problem?
   a. The problem is mine. I am the one who is upset. No one else in the relationship feels upset.
   b. The problem is yours. You are the one(s) who feel(s) upset. I (and others) do not feel upset.
   c. The problem is ours. We both (all) feel upset by what has taken place in our relationship.

If you checked Item A and feel that you must attempt to modify the other person's (or persons') behavior, try sending an I-message. (See the next section for further instructions.) If you checked Item B, use active listening with the student who feels upset. (See previous section for further instructions.) If you checked Item C, use the Six-Step Problem-Solving Method with the student involved in the relationship.

Table 7
Determining Your Response

SITUATION	WHO OWNS THE PROBLEM?	ACTIVE LISTENING	I-MESSAGE
Student crying about a low grade on a paper.	Student	You're feeling discouraged about your grades and maybe worried about what your parents will think of you.	
Student did not turn in assignment as agreed upon.	Teacher		When you don't keep agreements, I feel it's unfair because I cannot plan how to teach or reach you.
Student not able to answer or do the homework assignment.	Student	You're upset about the assignment and discouraged that you can't complete it.	
Student interrupts other students during a class discussion period.	Teacher		We can't talk with each other when you keep interrupting.
Student unhappy after losing a basketball game.	Student	You're pretty upset that you lost.	

Once the teacher decides who owns the problem, he is in a position to take action. If the student owns the problem, the teacher may decide (depending on the situation) to listen, to explore alternatives, or to allow the student to face the consequences independently. If the teacher discovers that he owns the problem, the courses of action in the next section will be open.

114

I-Messages

When the problem is the teacher's, she is the one who feels bothered. The students who bug her do not feel there is any problem. The students are *not* bothered. For example, let's say that several students are making considerable noise as they work together on a class project. The noise does not bother the students, but it does bother the teacher, who finds it difficult to concentrate and talk quietly with other students. The problem is the teacher's.

In order to influence the students, the teacher must communicate in such a way that her feelings, meanings, and intentions will be understood. Rather than ordering the noisy students to be quiet, which is a you-message, the teacher will be more effective sending an I-message, such as "I get annoyed when you talk so loud because I can't concentrate on what I'm doing." This statement avoids placing blame and making the students feel guilty or defensive, which undoubtedly would result if the teacher had said, "Will you *please* be quiet!"

The you-message lays blame and tends to criticize the student. It suggests that the student is at fault. It is simply a verbal attack. In contrast, an I-message simply describes how the student's behavior makes you feel. The message focuses on you, the teacher, and not on the student. It reports what you feel rather than assigning blame.

When a large number of students are simultaneously trying to get their needs met, it is not surprising that some become annoying, boisterous, inconsiderate, or stubborn. Teachers often feel overwhelmed and frustrated by the task of managing such a learning environment.

Following are examples of common situations in which the teacher owns the problem:

A student wastes art supplies.
A student leaves reference books and papers on the library table.
A student chews gum and leaves wrappers all over the place.
A student takes up a lot of your time tattling on other students.
Several students whisper loudly while you are giving directions.
A student is kicking a locker door.
A student uses materials from your desk without asking.

A student repeatedly comes late and disrupts the class when entering.

Several students argue loudly enough to interrupt you and the rest of the class.

A student doesn't return materials he has borrowed.

A student is about to pour juice over a cabinet.

Several students talk loudly during your conference with another student.

These and thousands of other student behaviors interfere with the teacher's legitimate needs and are unacceptable to most school professionals.

Educators have three variables with which to work when modifying unacceptable behavior:

1. Attempt to modify the student's behavior, such as asking a student to stop talking or confronting a student who persists in interrupting.
2. Attempt to modify the environment, such as providing the student with a different assignment or removing the student from the classroom.
3. Attempt to modify one's self, such as saying, "It's just a stage he'll grow out of soon" or "If the psychologist can't do any good, how can I?"

The first of these options deals with the I-message. The other two are covered in the section on Discipline and Classroom Management.

Most teachers attempt to modify students' behavior using messages that fit one of the following three categories:

1. *Solution messages:* These messages tell a student exactly how to modify his behavior—what he must do, had better do, should do, or might do. The teacher hands out solutions to his own problems and expects students to accept them. There are five different kinds of solution messages:
   a. Ordering, commanding, directing
      "Spit out that gum."
      "Sit down this minute."
   b. Warning, threatening
      "If you don't line up, I'll leave you standing out there all day."
      "One more time, young man, and you'll stay after school."
   c. Moralizing, preaching
      "You should know better than to do that."

"Fourth graders should know what is right."
d. Teaching, using logic, giving facts
   "Assignments don't get finished when you dawdle."
   "Books are for reading, not marking."
e. Advising, offering solutions
   "If I were you, I'd get back to work."
   "Visit during recess, not in class."

Many teachers think that messages like these are the quickest and most efficient way to get the student to change. The problem is that these messages seldom work, and even when they do, they contain a secret, hidden message that students resent: "You're too dumb to figure out how to help me."

2. *Put-down messages:* These messages always carry evaluation, criticism, ridicule, and judgment as they tear away at the student's character or self-image. There are six separate categories of put-down messages:
   a. Judging, criticizing, disagreeing, blaming
      "You're always the one who starts trouble here."
      "You're being naughty."
      "You're a pest."
   b. Name calling, stereotyping, ridiculing
      "You're acting like wild animals today."
      "You're a bunch of hippies.
   c. Interpreting, analyzing, diagnosing
      "You have problems with authority."
      "You're doing that to get attention."
   d. Praising, agreeing, giving positive evaluations
      "You have the brains to be a good student."
      "When you put forth the effort, you do such good work."
   e. Reassuring, sympathizing, supporting
      "It's hard to sit still on such a hot day, isn't it?"
      "I realize the game is tonight, but let's not forget you're in school until three o'clock."
   f. Probing, questioning, interrogating
      "Just why are you out of your seat?"
      "How do you expect to pass this course when you talk in class so much?"
      "Why didn't you put your materials back in the cupboard?"

Put-down messages may be either (1) discounted, in which case no positive behavior change occurs and the student makes inferences about the character of the teacher, or (2) internalized by the student as additional proof of his or her own inadequacy. Either way, the student hears the teacher sending the hidden

117

message, "There's something wrong with you or you wouldn't be causing me this problem!"

3. *Indirect messages:* This category includes kidding, teasing, sarcasm, digressions, and diverting comments.
   "Your shoes *look* better than they *sound.*"
   "I've never taught a class of monkeys before."
   "I suppose I'd be foolish to call on you today."
   "Could we wait for our little clown to stop showing off."
   "When did they make you principal of our school?"
   "I hope you grow up to be a teacher and have a hundred students like you."
   "We'll go on now that the comedy hour is over."

Such messages seldom work because they are usually not understood. Even when they are understood, students learn from them that the teacher is indirect and sneaky rather than direct and open. The hidden message is "If I confront you directly, you won't like me," or "It's too risky to be open and honest with you." Students then feel that the teacher is untrustworthy and manipulative.

Constructing an I-Message

I-messages meet three important criteria that make them more desirable than the previous messages: (1) they have a high probability of promoting a willingness to change, (2) they contain minimal negative evaluation of the student, and (3) they do not injure the relationship.

The I-message usually refers to three elements of a situation: feeling, behavior, and consequence. A simple formula using the following phrases is helpful in constructing I-messages:

1. "I feel . . ." (State your feeling about the consequence the behavior produces for you.)
2. "When you . . ." (Describe the behavior that is interfering with you. Do not blame, but rather convey in a nonjudgmental fashion.)
3. "Because . . ." (State the consequence the behavior has for you.)

Constrution of an I-message depends upon the situation. The parts of the message do not have to be stated in the above order, nor does an I-message always have to contain a statement of feeling. However, an effective I-message must focus on *you* rather than the student and must not place blame on anyone. Following are examples of I-messages.

> "I worry when you don't turn in your assignments, because I don't know where you are and cannot teach you."
>
> "I get angry when there is so much noise, because I cannot hear Matt's question."
>
> "Don, your being late to class is causing me a problem. When you come in late, I have to stop whatever I'm doing. It's distracting to me, and I'm frustrated."
>
> "When you have your feet in the aisle, I'm apt to trip over them, and I'm afraid I'll fall and get hurt."

Questions for Further Thought

1. Why is it important for you to focus on the problem-solving process and not just on solutions?
2. Give an example from your own teaching where you gave advice and where you explored alternatives.
3. What can a teacher do when a student is not able to generate ideas or alternatives?
4. Describe how problem ownership is a necessary concept for teachers to use.
5. List three I-messages that you gave (or could have given) today.

Exercise 1

The following are typical classroom situations. Determine who owns the problem.

1. A student says she is bored in your class.
2. A student gets angry in class, loses control, and starts yelling about how much he hates school, teachers, and especially you.
3. Your principal tells you that he expects you and every other teacher to attend the PTA meeting.

4. A student in your class frequently leaves reference books lying around the room rather than putting them back on the shelves where they belong.
5. A student in your high school biology class states that he has been smoking "grass" for several years and cannot stop.
6. A fellow staff member always takes out audio-visual materials without signing them out. When you need to use the equipment, you don't know where to find it.
7. A girl in your second grade class frequently cries when she doesn't get her way. This disrupts the entire classroom.
8. You like to come to school early and work, but when you do, other teachers come in and want to tell you all their problems.
9. A parent of one of your third-graders tells you that her child isn't learning to do math as well as the parent would like.
10. A student in your class complains that he doesn't have enough time to complete all the assigned work you have given him since he has an outside job that helps him to buy things his parents can't afford to provide.

Exercise 2

The following chart lists conflict situations in which only one person owns the problem. In Column II, write a typical you-message that might be sent in that situation. See the example provided for Situation 1. In Column III, write an I-message for each situation. See the example provided for Situation 1.

Use the three-step formula to help you. "I feel _____ when you _____ because I _____."

Avoid I-messages that are really disguised You-messages.

I. CONFLICT SITUATION	II. YOU-MESSAGE	III. I-MESSAGE
1. A teacher is upset with a student when she sits down and dawdles rather than doing the assignment.	"You'd better stop dawdling and get busy on your work or you'll miss recess again."	"I get upset when you don't do classroom work because I spend my time disciplining rather than teaching you."

I. CONFLICT SITUATION	II. YOU-MESSAGE	III. I-MESSAGE (con't)

2. The teacher promises to keep an eye on Jane's lunch while Jane runs an errand for her. When Jane returns, the teacher has stepped out of the room and part of Jane's lunch is missing.

3. Students working on a team project are so loud that others in the room are having difficulty working.

4. A student is upset because the other students refuse to let him in their game.

5. The teacher is talking with a student when another student interrupts the conversation for the third time.

6. Tom promises to return a book to Helen. After a friendly reminder, she again forgets the book.

Exercise 3

Read the following situations and construct an I-message for each.

1. You are conducting a parent conference while a group of students is playing noisily outside your window, thus making communication difficult.

2. For the last few days your class has been quite noisy; they have even been yelling to students in other classes on the way to the

cafeteria. The noise doesn't bother you particularly, but you know other teachers whose classes are still in session are getting upset. You decide to speak to your class about it before going to lunch today.

3. You are on playground duty and see a first-grader doing a handstand on the top of the slide.
4. Your fourth-grade students are working on independent art/social studies projects. Richard is wandering from desk to desk, talking to other students, getting drinks of water, sharpening pencils, and taking things from other student's desks.
5. You and your fifth-grade class decide to divide up the routine duties needed to operate an efficient class. For this week, Cindy has volunteered to empty the wastebaskets. The first two days she completed her job, but for the last days she has had to be reminded repeatedly.

Exercise 4

Use the six-step problem-solving process to figure out how you would resolve the following problems.

1. Mr. Tate thinks Sharon will slack off and stop working if he grades her too leniently. Sharon thinks Mr. Tate expects too much and grades her unfairly.
2. Mrs. Harris feels that John will take advantage of her if she is not tough on him in class. John feels that Mrs. Harris is too strict and is forcing him to find devious ways to meet his need for independence and autonomy.
3. Linda and Anne share a locker. Linda likes to keep all of her books and projects, a change of clothing, make-up, and other assorted items in her locker because it is so handy. Anne likes to keep only a few essential books and her coat in the locker so that it won't be messy. Each is upset by the other.
4. Mary and Bill are working together on a project. Mary feels that Bill is not contributing his share to the project. Bill feels that Mary is too bossy and won't let him contribute to the project in the way he thinks is best. They are at an impasse.
5. Jill and Larry both need to use the tape recorder for several days. Each has selected a project that involves interviewing a number

of students in the class and taping their responses. Jill wants to find out how her classmates feel about ecology. Larry wants to find out how his classmates feel about population control. There is not enough time before the projects are due for each of them to have a turn at the tape recorder. Thus, they have decided to do a joint project that combines questions about ecology and population control. However, Jill feels that Larry's questions are too detailed. Larry feels that Jill is just skimming the surface. Each is upset with the other, and valuable time is passing by quickly.

References

COMBS, A. W., D. AVILA, and W. W. PURKEY. *Helping Relationships.* Boston: Allyn and Bacon, 1971.

DINKMEYER, D., and G. D. McKAY. *Systematic Training for Effective Parenting: Parent's Handbook.* Circle Pines, MN: American Guidance Service, 1976.

GORDON, T. *Teacher Effectiveness Training.* New York: Peter Wyden, 1974.

HOWE, L. W., and M. M. HOWE. *Personalizing Education: Values Clarification and Beyond.* New York: Hart, 1975.

8

Working Together

Despite the fact that most teaching takes place in a group setting, many teachers have little training in group leadership. Teachers are trained to teach individuals. We have become so indoctrinated with "the individual" in the educational situation that we tend to think of the one-to-one relationship of the teacher with the child as the primary relationship.

The key to effective group facilitation is learning to work *with* groups rather than *against* them.

Not too many years ago, the teachers and the principal in the school largely determined the behavior of the students, as did the parents in the family. These authorities had the power to enforce conformity to the rules. The teacher set the goals, asked the questions, called on students to answer, responded to the answer, and made the decisions. Adult society supported the standard for the authoritarian figure.

As we have become more democratic, adult dominance has been replaced by the peer group. Individual authority has diminished—it no longer works. Students today are more concerned about peer approval than about adult approval. Students feel free to express rebellion and defiance.

Group Dynamics

Teachers can become more effective by developing skills for dealing with the class as a group. Students are social beings; they want to belong to a group. When they are part of a group, they feel secure.

Students create their identity within the classroom by their behavior. The goals they adopt express their beliefs about how they belong to the group. Students seek their place in accordance with their concept of themselves and of life, while simultaneously assuming specific roles within a group. Because students may have mistaken goals, the classroom can be a place of conflict and competition rather than peace and cooperation.

Although most teachers have at least a vague idea about the principles of group dynamics, actually helping a group develop is a tremendous challenge. Some teachers give in to the pressures and expectations of the group. Others find a way to use the group as a means of fostering cooperation, support, and encouragement.

A classroom full of students is not necessarily a group. A collection of individuals must develop skills for working together cooperatively in order to become an effective working unit.

Group dynamics helps us understand why students seek mistaken goals such as attention, power, revenge, or why they display inadequacy. As teachers come to understand the group, they can direct students' energies toward cooperation and useful behavior.

Effective classroom groups don't just happen. They develop slowly under the skillful supervision of a dedicated teacher. The time you spend working on the students' social and psychological growth can directly affect their willingness to learn, lessen discipline problems, and promote their personal growth.

Once you gain the respect of the group, you can encourage students to help those who misbehave to find a place in a positive way. Students who feel they belong and are accepted work together. They have no need to establish significance by misbehaving.

There is great joy in teaching a group in which the students and teacher care about each other and work together. Every teacher is capable of building a socially interested class that cooperates, encourages each other, works for the good of the group, and demonstrates mutual respect.

Unite the Class

Teachers needn't be psychologists in order to deal with the feelings, values, and attitudes of the students. Perhaps there is nothing more important that a teacher can do to facilitate helpful behavior than uniting the class and taking a place as a member of the united group.

It is important not only for you to accept the students as they are, but also for them to accept each other. Mutual respect and empathy will blossom as the students learn to listen and respond to their peers.

Students are used to the traditional classroom in which they are supposed to pay attention only to the teacher. As they become aware of the feelings of the other students, a more accepting atmosphere develops. You can encourage empathy among students by pointing out occasions in which they are tuning in to one another: "Shelly, I've noticed your concern about how Diane is feeling."

Students need to feel free to express their thoughts, feelings, and values. Anger can be reduced by talking with someone who cares. Teachers can model ventilation by using an I-message such as, "I feel discouraged when there is a lot of talking while I'm trying to teach because I'm afraid we won't finish this chapter by Friday."

Encourage students to express their feelings about events such as losing a ball game, seeing someone cheat on an exam, and other situations in which they may feel positive or negative feelings.

Work toward replacing competition with cooperation. You might ask students what they do well that they would be willing to help others do. Point out and encourage spontaneous altruism, such as, "Lisa, I appreciate your helping Kristen with the spelling words," or "That was thoughtful of you to take Tom's assignment home to him when he was sick."

As members of the group share the way they've solved problems, other students learn how to deal with their own dilemmas. Sometimes students don't have enough courage to discuss their problems but can learn from a classmate's discussion of a similar problem. You could ask the group: "How else might you have done that?" or "What did you learn from Sally's way of dealing with the problem?"

Students who interact only with the teacher are not learning how to function socially outside the classroom. You may want to reexamine the value of silence in class, giving weight to interaction with each other. Encourage students to speak directly to each other in class. For example: "Sam, please talk directly to Dawn when you are commenting on something she has said." It is also helpful to create opportunities for students to work together without your supervision.

Encourage

Students grow to believe in themselves and their abilities in an atmosphere of encouragement. There is no healthier, more effective learning environment than one based on encouragement.

Focusing on strengths and acknowledging effort as well as contribution build courage within students. Marking the right answers rather than the wrong and developing realistic expectations are avenues of encouragement. By modeling encouragement, teachers can do a lot toward increasing students' self-esteem and teaching them how to increase the self-confidence of each other.

A weekly "Encouragement Day" is a good way of getting students to think in a positive way. You choose a topic, such as "A time when someone helped me feel good about myself." The teacher may begin by sharing an experience. For example, "A student told me that he likes my sense of humor. Who else will tell us about a time when they were encouraged?" Then each student has a chance to tell about one trait they like about themselves. Encouragement Day directs peer pressure in a positive way.

It is often difficult for students to deal with positive statements about themselves. You might point out that there is something very special about each student in the classroom. Recognizing that specialness helps us feel good about ourselves. The following week you might discuss "Something I like about someone else in the class."

Another idea is to have an Encouragement Box, in which students' names are placed. On Encouragement Day everyone, including the teacher, draws a name. Each person then writes an encouraging statement on the back of the slip of paper about the person she has drawn. These "Encouragement Gifts" are then distributed to the owner.

A bit of encouragement from an understanding teacher can change a person's life. Your students are itching to be noticed. Your understanding and patience can convert a classroom of students into a productive, working group.

Effective classroom groups share certain characteristics:

1. The members understand, acknowledge, and accept one another.
2. Communication is open and honest.
3. Members take responsibility for their own learning and behavior.
4. Members value cooperation.
5. Members are able to confront problems openly and resolve their conflicts constructively. (Stanford, 1980).

Group Skills for Teachers

Although a democratic classroom promotes active participation by the students, the teacher's guidance and direction are essential. Your style of leadership is a critical part of an effective group. The following skills will be helpful in creating successful discussion within the group. (Dinkmeyer, McKay, and Dinkmeyer, Jr., 1980)

Structuring. Ask the class to help you formulate guidelines. These are necessary in order to keep the group on the subject being discussed. Once guidelines are established, the teacher has a way to let students know how they may be departing from the agreed upon procedures.

Guidelines can be rules such as raise your hand, listen carefully, stick to the point, don't interrupt, tell how you feel, and be positive. Once you and the students agree upon the guidelines, it is wise to post them for reference. Then when someone speaks out without raising his or her hand, or discusses the football game instead of the subjects and predicates, you can ask, "Which guidelines are we forgetting?"

Universalizing. Careful listening and a cohesive group develop as students discover they have a lot in common. Terry says, "I hate to do homework on weekends." Tim says, "I do too." What these students have in common binds them together.

You can encourage universalization by asking questions such as, "How many of you have experienced this? Who else has felt that way? How many of you feel nervous about taking exams?"

Linking. Pointing out similarities and differences in opinions, values, and beliefs promotes closeness among students. Teachers can facilitate discussions by verbally making connections between different people. For example, "Phil gets very upset when his brother doesn't return what he borrows. This seems similar to what Kathy and Peggy feel about their sisters."

Redirecting. Students are encouraged to get involved in discussions when the teacher redirects questions or statements back to the class: "What does someone think about that?" Redirecting also creates a more democratic environment because it allows the teacher to step out of the role of authority figure.

When Mike says, "It's really tough to be the youngest child," you can ask the group, "How do the rest of you feel about that?" If a student offers an unworkable solution, the teacher can ask, "What might happen if we try that?"

Goal disclosing. Revealing the goal helps students become aware of the purpose of their misbehavior. This must be done in a sensitive, caring manner so as not to trap or embarrass the student.

You might ask Matt if he would like to learn why he walks around the room during class. If he appears interested, ask the class to guess why Matt might be doing this. When someone suggests a possibility, ask the group, "Does everyone agree? Matt, what do you think about that idea?"

If no one has an idea, you could suggest a possibility, beginning with, "Could it be . . . ?" or "I have the impression . . ." Then state the goal such as, "You want us to pay attention to you." If Matt's recognition reflex suggests that you are correct, you might get into a discussion on other ways students can be noticed. This takes the pressure off Matt. You might, however, first check out with Matt how he feels about the suggestion.

Brainstorming. Sharing ideas without screening them encourages creative thinking. Invite the students to share their ideas about a problem. Tell them there are no right and wrong answers and no evaluations will be made until all the suggestions are given.

For example, ask the students what to do about noise in the cafeteria during lunch period. Or you might ask them why spelling correctly is important or what suggestions they have to help Todd solve his problems.

Blocking. Should a discussion turn into an attack, it becomes necessary for the teacher to intervene. You can block the remarks by telling the students that the group won't accept such comments, or you can suggest the students use I-messages to state their feelings. If Chuck says, "We don't want you on our team. You always make us lose," the teacher can ask Chuck to be specific about what bothers him by expressing his feeling in the form of an I-message.

Summarizing. The teacher can summarize by saying, "So far we've learned . . ." This helps to clarify the discussion. Teaching students to summarize is especially valuable, because it reveals to you what they are learning. Beginning with "I learned . . . ," the students' summaries can focus on content, feelings, beliefs, or attitudes.

Setting tasks and obtaining commitments. It's easier to talk about a solution to a problem than to take action to solve it. Teachers can encourage students to develop specific commitments for action. After Bill and the class discuss his failing Spanish grade, you might say, "Bill, what do you plan to do this week about improving your Spanish grade?" Alignment of goals is critical so that students and teachers can work together.

Promoting feedback. Feedback is an important skill in which you tell another person the kind of impact that person's behavior is having on you. Based on honesty, feedback helps people understand how others perceive them. I-messages are the most effective way of providing feedback in a nonthreatening way.

For example, "I feel hurt when you tease me about my weight because I know I'm too fat." Or "I feel discouraged when students come unprepared for history class because the discussion is carried on by just a few students. How do the rest of you feel?"

Promoting direct interaction. Group discussions are more effective when students speak directly to each other. For example, "Mark, please tell Paul how you feel about what he said."

Promoting encouragement. Encouragement is contagious. Recognize the efforts of your students as well as their contributions. Teachers can encourage as well as teach their students to encourage.

You might ask, "Who has noticed Jack's effort to be on time this week?" You might say, "I like the way you helped each other figure out the problem."

Group Learning

Group learning activities are effective when used as an integral part of the curriculum. Avoid the use of group activities as a gimmick tacked on as an afterthought. Teachers who are effective with groups are those who give as much attention and effort to the development of the class as a group as they give to individual mastery of skills in subject matter.

SKILL	PURPOSE	EXAMPLE
Structuring	To establish purpose and limits for discussion.	"What's happening in the group now?" How is this helping us reach our goal?"
Universalizing	To help students realize that their concerns are shared.	"Who else has felt that way?"
Linking	To make verbal connections between what specific students say and feel.	"Bill is very angry when his brother is late. This seems similar to what Joan and Sam feel about their sisters."
Redirecting	To promote involvement of all students in the discussion and to allow teachers to step out of the role of authority figure.	"What do others think about that" "What do you think about Pete's idea?"
Goal disclosure	To help students become more aware of the purposes of their misbehavior.	"Is it possible you want us to notice you?" "Could it be you want to show us we can't force you?"
Brainstorming	To encourage students to participate unhesitatingly in generating ideas.	"Let's share all our ideas about this problem. We won't react to any suggestion until we've listed them all."
Blocking	To intervene in destructive communication.	"Will you explain your feelings?" "I wonder how Stanley felt when you said that."
Summarizing	To clarify what has been said and to determine what students have learned.	"What did you learn from this discussion?" What have we decided to do about this situation?"
Task setting and obtaining commitments	To develop a specific commitment for action from students.	"What will you do about this problem?" "What will you do this week?"

Group Leadership Skills (continued)

SKILL	PURPOSE	EXAMPLE
Promoting feedback	To help students understand how others perceive them.	"I get angry when you talk so long that the rest of us don't get a turn. What do the others think?" "I really like the way you help us get our game started."
Promoting direct interaction	To get students to speak directly to each other when appropriate.	"Would you tell Joan how you feel about what she said?"
Promoting encouragement	To invite students directly and by example to increase each other's self-esteem and self-confidence.	"Thank you for helping us out." "What does Carol do that you like?" "Who has noticed Jamie's improvement?"

(D. Dinkmeyer, G. D. McKay, & D. Dinkmeyer, Jr. *Systematic Training For Effective Teaching,* p. 206, Circle Pines, MN: American Guidance Service, 1980.)

Group guidance as experiential learning tends to be valued and retained. Learning strategies can take various forms, such as art, discussions, music, role-playing, writing, field trips, and games. The focus of activities is on attitudes, feelings, beliefs, and goals, as well as on self-image and human relationships.

Group guidance is preventive and developmental in that issues are discussed *before* they become problems. Identifying individual strengths, setting goals, aligning the goals of students and teacher, building self-confidence, and nurturing cooperation are essential elements of effective guidance.

Education is not just the accumulation of information. A student's academic success is influenced by the *context* of learning. Those who learn in a mistake-centered classroom are apt to have negative ideas about their subjects. If students learn in an atmosphere of support, safety, success, and encouragement, chances are they will be good students and enjoy learning. Our feelings about what we learn can determine how quickly and how much we learn.

Over time, the interest, involvement, support, and acceptance of the group become more important than that of the teacher. Consequently, learning depends less on the teacher's approval and more on the personal desire of the student to be a valuable member of the group.

Group Activities

A **class discussion** is often an effective way for students to learn in a group setting. Students can sit in a circle, talking to each other as well as to the teacher. You can stimulate discussion and learning by asking thought-provoking questions.

Perhaps you are discussing someone cutting in front of you to get into line. You might get the group started by asking questions such as:

"How do you feel when someone cuts in front of you in line?"

"What do you do when this happens?"

"What might work better?"

You might decide to assign a somewhat controversial topic such as, "How does ability affect success?" Encourage all members to listen carefully to what each has to say, as well as to contribute their own opinions.

Students often enjoy **role-playing** activities. You give them a problem to act out, such as how it feels to be a new student at school. Ask for volunteers to play the parts: new student, other students, teacher. Discuss each part and then leave it up to the role-players to behave as they think their characters would.

After the scene is acted out, discuss the feelings and motivations of each character. Determine if the audience (other students) understood what the actor was trying to convey. Ask the actors how it felt to be in their particular role. Ask the audience how it felt to watch the scene.

Role-playing makes students aware of the feelings and goals of others, as well as pointing out alternative ways to behave.

Interesting **pictures** clipped from magazines and newspapers often promote lively discussions. The valuable part of

134

this activity is that of seeing the students' perceptions. What the picture really shows doesn't matter. This is especially effective if the pictures point to feelings, attitudes, and values.

You might ask, "How do you think the person in the picture feels? How would you feel if you were in such a situation?"

Exercises and games can be nonthreatening ways of learning about communication, feelings, and motivation. Numerous examples can be found in Gene Stanford's *Developing Effective Classroom Groups* (1980). Following are a few examples.

1. *Seeking allies:* Go around the circle asking students to name another member of the group they think they are most similar to.
2. *Acting out:* Tell the students to pantomime something that tells about them, such as a hobby, a special talent, or something they like to do.
3. *Sentence stems:* Give each student a copy of sentence stems, such as the following. Ask them to complete the sentences in writing. They can share their answers with a partner, a small group, or the whole class.

> I like . . .
> Sometimes I wish . . .
> Whenever I make a poor grade . . .
> I can't . . .
> When I was younger . . .
> Most people know . . .
> I need to know . . .
> Whenever I enter a new group . . .
> I regret . . .
> My goal . . .
> I'm afraid . . .
> It makes me proud when I . . .
> A good thing that happened recently was . . .

Art, music, and **writing** can be used to demonstrate feelings. Ask the students to draw a picture of their family or their home. Some may enjoy writing a poem or a story.

Guest speakers and **field trips** are often popular learning activities.

Establishing Democratic Class Leadership

Class meetings are an important part of a democratic classroom. The entire class meets at a specific time each week to share ideas, feelings, opinions, and plans. Everyone functions as an equal as students encourage and help each other. A democratic classroom fosters cooperation, empathy, and trust.

Planning is one of the most important functions of a class meeting. Although there are school matters students cannot decide, there are always some opportunities for students to work with the teacher in setting guidelines and deciding policies. Alternative ways of grading, assigning classroom jobs, changing the curriculum, and doing projects for extra credit are among areas that can be discussed by students as well as teachers.

Students could be asked to submit test questions or ideas for the science fair. When we give students an opportunity to plan their learning, we also give them a chance to assume responsibility for their learning.

Problem solving is another critical element of a class meeting. It is more effective to have the class help in solving behavior problems than to impose a solution yourself. The class develops certain expectations, and those who do not live up to them realize that their behavior is not acceptable to the group. The class can encourage a misbehaving student to find a place in a more acceptable way.

The misbehaving student may be given the choice of discussing the situation with the group, stopping his misbehavior, or having the class help decide how to deal with the misbehavior.

Problem solving often reveals to misbehaving students that they are not alone in their feelings and that the group disapproves not of them as persons but only of their response to the feelings—their behavior.

Students may wish to discuss problems involving the whole group or troublesome relationships with parents, teachers, or friends. The class meeting provides a time for the group to offer encouragement and suggestions.

Perhaps nothing is more important at a class meeting than **encouragement.** Always emphasize the positive. Look for strengths. For example, "How many of you have noticed how Jeff has improved in his reading? Let's see how we can work this problem out together."

Take a few moments at the beginning of each class meeting for Good News time. "I have some good news today about Scott. He has handed in his homework on time every day this week."

Soon students will share their "good news."

You might begin the class meeting by asking the students, "What is positive and new in your life?"

Running Class Meetings

It takes patience, commitment, and time to get to the point where class meetings run smoothly. Take a seat within the circle so that you are an equal part of the group and listen closely to what each student says.

The purpose of the class meeting is to bring about change. It is not a gripe session. Encourage the students to help each other and to make everyone feel accepted. If someone brings up a complaint, you might say, "Ginger, I appreciate the subject you've brought to light. Who has an idea on how we might solve this problem?"

Class meetings can be used to discuss the goals of misbehavior. Students can learn to detect the real issues behind what people say and do. If you notice some students vying for attention, discuss how people use the goal of attention.

Class meetings give students an opportunity to practice clear speaking and careful listening. If the discussion keeps wandering back to someone's complaints, redirect the conversation by saying, "I wonder why we're having trouble staying on the topic?"

Work toward consensus. If at all possible, delay decisions until all students agree. The problem with going by majority rule is that the minority may be uncooperative.

If time is running out, it may be necessary for the teacher to make the decision. Students who disagree may offer their suggestions at the following meeting. Unfinished business goes on the agenda for the next meeting. It is also helpful to have an Agenda Box in which students place their suggestions for the upcoming meeting.

Initiating Class Meetings

When introducing your students to class meetings, it is helpful to keep in mind the following points.

Arrange seats in a circle. It is wise to start out by discussing low-key issues such as classroom jobs and field trips. Students learn to make decisions by making them. Give the group an opportunity to make some choices.

The teacher might say, "It seems like I've been making most of the decisions about what happens in our classroom. Let's talk about how we can work together to get the jobs done. How can we divide the work fairly?"

Once the class is used to taking responsibility, you can give them the opportunity to make decisions on more complicated issues. It is a good idea to offer young children two choices, such as, "Would you like to draw your pictures in the morning or afternoon?"

When you feel that your students are ready, introduce problem solving by enlisting the help of the class on a specific problem. Cooperation and cohesiveness will increase as students work on problems together.

Once the students have worked through a number of problems, you can set up regular class meetings. Make some suggestions about planning an agenda, establishing rules for discussion, and setting the time and length of meetings.

If you decide to be the chairperson for the first few class meetings, sit in a different place in the circle for each meeting to demonstrate the equality of all participants.

Once the formal class meetings have been established, it is important to stick to time limits, not to skip meetings, to block personal attacks, and to prevent the meeting from becoming a gripe session.

Some teachers have difficulty becoming an equal group member. If you dominate discussions and make rules, the class meeting loses its purpose. Listen to what the students are saying and give them the opportunity to experience responsibility.

Exercises and Activities

Following are some games that help students work together.

Who Are Your Neighbors?
Seat students in a large circle, instructing them to learn the

names of the people on the other side of them. Ask for a volunteer to be "it" who stands in the middle of the circle. "It" walks up to any player and asks, "Who are your neighbors?" If a player does not answer correctly, she becomes "it" and the former "it" takes her place, learning the neighbor's names before the game proceeds.

If the player answers correctly, "it" asks, "Do you want new neighbors?" If the player answers yes, the whole group changes seats, with "it" taking someone's seat, leaving the player without a chair as the new "it." Each time the students change places, they learn the names of their neighbors before continuing the game. (Stanford, 1980)

Forced Choice
Move desks to the side so as to leave a large empty space in the center. Ask a question that requires students to make an either/or decision, such as, "Would you rather live in Hawaii or New York? Are you a leader or a follower?"

Instruct students who take one position to move to one side of the room, and those who take the other to move to the opposite side. No one is allowed to "straddle the fence." Point out that we often face decisions in life where neither alternative seems better than the other.

Once the students have moved to their chosen side of the room, have them look around to see how others have voted. If time is sufficient, students may find a partner on their side of the room and discuss why they made the choice they did.

Questions can deal with opinions and personal qualities or relate to issues of subject matter. For example:

If you had a choice between a job in a big city with bad air pollution or one in a rural area where the nearest town was forty miles away, which would you choose?

Would you rather watch television or go to a movie?

Which would you rather be, president of Ford Motor Company or a U.S. senator?

Do you like to spend your time with lots of people around or are you happier alone?

Would you rather attend a symphony concert or a boxing match?

Are you a leader or a follower?

Would you have fought for the Arabs or the Israelis in the 1973 war?

Which can you tolerate better, a classroom that is ten degrees too hot, or one that is ten degrees too cold?

(Simon, 1972)

Magic Shop

Seat the class in a circle, giving the following instructions: "I want you to imagine that I am the proprietor of a magic shop—a place where you can exchange a personal characteristic you have but don't like for one you'd rather have. For example, you can offer to trade me your tendency to talk about people behind their backs for the ability to control your temper." Go around the circle giving every student a chance to make a trade in the shop. Do not allow questions or discussion until all students have had an opportunity to respond. (Stanford, 1980)

Restating

Arrange the class in a circle, either as a total group or in small groups. Assign a controversial issue to be discussed. Require students to summarize the previous student's remarks before adding their own contributions. Appoint one or two students to monitor the discussions and interrupt any students who do not satisfactorily summarize the previous contribution before adding their own. (Stanford, 1980)

Visiting Celebrity

Explain to the class that you will be playing a game similar in format to the television shows *Meet the Press* or *Face the Nation.* Ask for a volunteer to be interviewed, and tell the rest of the class they are the reporters. The students take turns asking questions to find out what kind of person the interviewee is. The student being interviewed has the option of responding to any question with "no comment" if she or he prefers not to answer. (Stanford, 1980)

A Symphony of Needs

The teacher invites each student to list seven needs he is aware of having. For example:

1. I need someone to love me.
2. I need to lose weight.

140

3. I need to feel accepted by the other students.
4. I need to get better grades.
5. I need more time to study.
6. I need more freedom than my parents give me.
7. I need my own car.

After each student completes his list, the teacher invites the group to form a circle. A volunteer who is willing to share his list of needs sits in the center of the circle. The volunteer chooses seven other students, assigning one of his needs to each.

An additional student is selected by the volunteer to serve as a "conductor." Much as a symphony conductor directs an orchestra, the conductor brings in one or more of the seven selected, who state the need that they were assigned.

The conductor spends two or three minutes on the symphony of needs. A period of silence follows, during which the volunteer continues to remain in the circle with eyes closed, checking out his awarenesses. The volunteer then shares with the group anything he noticed. The activity continues until everyone has participated. (Anderson, 1977)

Me-in-a-Box

The students must receive advance instruction to bring with them five articles or symbols (in a box) that represent meaningful experiences or prized possessions.

The teacher invites the students to form a circle. Each then shares with the group the five articles she brought.

The articles may represent friendships, accomplishments, positions, work, artistic creations, fond memories, or special interests. As the students participate in this activity, they reveal a great deal of information about themselves.

When each student has had a chance to share, the teacher concludes the activity by asking, "Who has noticed anything or was surprised in any way?" (Anderson, 1977)

Summary

Teachers can become more effective by working with the class as a group. However, merely choosing group interaction as a method is not enough. It is only the beginning of a long and difficult process of developing skills for dealing with the class as a group.

Students learn how to deal with their own problems as they hear other group members share the way they've solved their dilemmas. Students grow to believe in themselves in an atmosphere of encouragement. Teachers can learn group leadership skills that will promote discussion within the group. Group learning activities can be an enriching part of the curriculum. Class meetings are important in a democratic classroom.

Every teacher is capable of building a socially interested class that cooperates, encourages each other, works for the good of the group, and demonstrates mutual respect. Guiding the development of a group into a mature working unit can bring rich dividends. Students develop priceless skills that can enhance their lives for years to come.

Questions for Further Thought

1. How does skill in group dynamics help your teaching?
2. How can you replace competition in the classroom with cooperation?
3. How can you use encouragement to build a cohesive group in the classroom?
4. Why is it helpful to involve the class in dealing with behavior problems?
5. What would you see as advantages to having classroom meetings?
6. What do you find challenging about leading a classroom discussion democratically?

References

ANDERSEN, J. *Human Relations: An Experiential Facilitative Approach*. Ankeny, IA: Heartland Education Agency, 1977.
DINKMEYER, D., G. D. MCKAY, and D. DINKMEYER, JR. *Systematic Training for Effective Teaching*. Circle Pines, MI: American Guidance Service, 1980.

DREIKURS, R., B. GRUNWALD, and F. PEPPER. *Maintaining Sanity in the Classroom*, 2nd ed. New York: Harper & Row, 1980.

STANFORD, G. *Developing Effective Classroom Groups*. New York: Hart, 1977.

WALTON, F.X., and R.L. POWERS. *Winning Children Over*. Chicago: Practical Psychology Associates, 1978.

Additional Resources

CANFIELD, J., and H. WELLS. *100 Ways to Enhance Self-Concept in the Classroom*. Englewood Cliffs, NJ: Prentice-Hall, 1976

DINKMEYER, D., and J. MORO. *Group Counseling: Theory and Practice*, 2nd ed. Itasca, IL: F. E. Peacock, 1979.

SIMON, S., L. HOWE, and H. KIRSCHENBAUM. *Values Clarification*. New York: A & W Publishers, 1972.

Index